GIRLS WHO BECAME ARTISTS

GIRLS
WHO BECAME
ARTISTS

BY

WINIFRED AND FRANCES
KIRKLAND

Essay Index Reprint Series

BOOKS FOR LIBRARIES PRESS, INC.
FREEPORT, NEW YORK

First published 1934
Reprinted 1967

LIBRARY OF CONGRESS CATALOG CARD NUMBER:

67-26753

PRINTED IN THE UNITED STATES OF AMERICA

CONTENTS

GIRLS WHO BECAME ARTISTS

CHAPTER I

WANDA GAG,
WHO FOLLOWED HER OWN WAY

WHEN, some thirty-odd years ago, Wanda Gag's parents came to New Ulm, Minnesota, they brought with them all Bohemia. But they brought little else. The two proceeded to present their adopted country with a lot of lively little new citizens, a string of girls and one boy. Wanda was the eldest. Today she is known to the world as one of the most original of America's women artists. It is worth while to look back into her past to discover what influences have gone to making Wanda Gag the gifted, whimsical craftsman she is today.

Wanda Gag is a person who, with all sorts of circumstances piling up to thwart her, has succeeded in being—and quite happily—herself. Always she has seen her own special path beckoning her, and has followed it. The first thing to note about her childhood is that while actually Wanda Gag was born and reared in Minnesota, she knew little more about this country than if she had been brought up in the moon. Her parents, her neighbors, her whole village, were Bohemian. New Ulm kept all the Old World ways. It might just as well have been located in the heart of Hungary. These immigrants who had built a home village for themselves here in the Middle West all came of sturdy peasant stock. But there is nothing stodgy about Bohemian peasants. They know how to sing, they know how to paint, they know how to tell stories. For centuries they have delighted in doing all these things, and when a group of them migrated to New Ulm they brought with them their keen artistic sense. This enthusiasm for all art might express itself in quaint, Old World forms, but it was very real and burning just the same. New Ulm might be in all externals a raw, newly settled little town, but its children were nursed on traditions that were centuries old. Along with the other youngsters of the place, the little Gags, all seven of them, listened to old songs and to the music of the zither, saw and shared folk dances that in other spots had been long forgotten, learned to shudder at whispered superstitions, sat breathless while grown-ups told once more the old German *Märchen*, folk tales handed down from one generation to the next. It is no wonder that Wanda Gag says of herself, "My background, although I have never left this country, is European."

With their awakening imaginations already stirred by all the rich lore long accumulated in old Bohemia and now imported into modern Minnesota, the Gag children had certain other great advantages within their own home. It was a very humble home and always poverty-stricken. But in it children sang and danced and drew and painted from dawn to dark. Heavily burdened as they were, two parents shared with them every delight. A father and mother, themselves artistic to the core, managed somehow very early to convey to their offspring the idea that children must carry on when the parents are forced to stop. In father and mother alike there was the strongest urge to artistic expression, but neither one had had any chance for training, so the mother's love of color went to the making of gay frocks for her little girls, and the father's to the frescoing of bright angels on the ceilings of country churches. For six days of the week he toiled away as wall-painter and house decorator, but on the seventh all the household shared his glee when he entered his attic studio, and there, all Sunday long, painted what he pleased.

All the Gags took to drawing from babyhood on to their teens, and didn't stop then. Wanda, the most gifted of them all, supposed that all families were the same as hers, as ready to draw as to eat. She was to learn later the differences between the Gags and other youngsters; for presently the little group was to stand alone, but all as if one, solidly together, shoulder to shoulder, against the world. Their chief bulwark and defense was to be that delight in beauty, that joy in craftsmanship, which had been their baby inheritance. Both father and mother were radiant in spirit, but in the struggles and hardships both were fighting a losing battle in health. Tuberculosis laid its hold on the father, and after a year in bed he passed from them. He was laid to rest on the seventh baby's first birthday. The mother dragged on bravely. She held out against the neighbors who would have had Wanda, now fourteen, put to work as clerk in a grocery store. Instead the girl somehow managed to get away for a year's art instruction in Minneapolis and St. Paul.

Her ability showed itself at once and won her a scholarship for study in New York. But in the present circumstances it was quite impossible to make use of this opportunity, so Wanda Gag returned to New Ulm, to teach there for a year. She was still only in her later teens when her mother slipped away after the father.

Now comes the story of sheer, unbreakable pluck, the story of how a family of orphans played "follow my leader." Down to the last little toddler all stood together and all stood by Wanda. Wanda looked the situation straight in the eye and made two resolutions—she would not desert her family, neither would she desert the artist's career that lay before her. Whatever happened, Wanda Gag was going to be herself. If she looked in one direction she saw a line of little sisters, descending step by step to the littlest of all. If she looked in the other she saw gleaming that scholarship at the Art Students' League, New York, still waiting for her.

The first thing the young Gags had to resist was the neighbors. The neighbors would have put the youngest three into an orphanage. No, said the Gags; first and foremost they would not be separated. Next they would get themselves educated—somehow! They made a resolve, and turned it into a slogan, "High School for All!" And to that slogan they stuck, until the very last one of them had graduated. There followed years as determined as they were difficult. Although the eldest of them all was still well this side of twenty, the older ones went to work, teaching, painting place cards, making lamp shades. There was a long stretch when the sisters did without breakfast, so that a rapidly growing small brother might have his fill. The seven had as assets the house they lived in and the father's life insurance of a thousand dollars. This last they divided into five parts and made each two hundred last a year. The county allowed them twelve dollars a month in groceries. The baker allowed them, for a dime a day, a bagful of stale rolls. A houseful of youngsters learned the virtues of cornmeal mush. They learned how to stretch a penny to the vanishing-point. But in their fine-drawn budget they never allowed for dress, for they all went clad in hand-me-downs. While they couldn't accept advice from the neighbors, they could and did accept cast-off clothes—remade, for the Gag girls were born with clever fingers. They don't seem to have been in the least sorry for themselves. Of course, after all, they had one another, and they had Wanda. They worked, they went to school, but they never stopped drawing and dreaming.

At last came the day on which Wanda had always counted. Always, sooner or later, she meant to be herself. Being herself meant, first of all, being a sister to the brood of younger ones left to her. But just as soon as that brood could stand on its own feet, being herself meant being an artist. Exactly in proportion as their thousand dollar inheritance had been growing smaller, the Gag children had been growing bigger. When the last dollar in their bank account came in sight, Wanda up and sold the house and moved the family to Minneapolis. They could have better opportunities there, she felt, both for earning money and for getting an education. She watched while promptly they all fell on their feet. Almost overnight the transplanted household was running smoothly. The money from the sale of the house in New Ulm was sternly kept for rent, fuel, and light, for these only. Sisters Two and Three proceeded to earn the rest of the family living by typing, decorating cards, creating lamp shades. Sister Four, just graduated, did the housework. The remaining members were still obeying the family slogan, "High School for All." Once again Wanda looked the situation in the eye, in one direction seeing a line of capable younger sisters, in the other that scholarship still beckoning. Then she went to New York to begin her career.

It wasn't easy in New York. It is not easy to batter one's way to a career in the biggest and loneliest city in the world. Wanda needed those letters from Minneapolis, cheery, racy letters that arrived every day. They helped her to carry on during that first year of study at the Art Students' League. When that year was finished, she had to turn to lamp shades again, and to anything else she could lay her hand on, in order to retain her foothold in the great city. But Wanda Gag's hand was too gifted to be empty long, and commercial art offered a prompt reward, little as the soul of an artist desired to do fashion plates. Fashion plates paid, however. The letters to Minneapolis began to enclose checks, larger and larger checks.

Wanda Gag was now becoming more and more successful, as far as money means success. But she was far from being satisfied. New York had proved to be no road of roses. She had plenty of hard knocks, and survived them. She even had her first love-affair, and survived that, too. But she was lonely and homesick and disillusioned. She was not sure that drawing fashion sheets was really being an artist. After all, here in New York she was not sure she was being herself. Meanwhile out in Minneapolis the other Gags had not for a day stopped saving and working and studying. But now the youngest of them had at last finished high school. There was no reason for further separation. Wanda sent for her family and packed them into a happy little apartment in the East Seventies.

Now Wanda Gag was at last free to look where all artists' dreams lead—across the water to Europe. The money to go kept mounting; it reached fourteen hundred dollars. Then in a flash an unfortunate business venture wiped out one thousand of this sum. There was no use traveling off for European study with only four hundred dollars in one's purse. So Wanda gave up Europe. But with no vain repining! The Gags are not that sort. When they can't do one thing, they do something else. Later, Wanda Gag was able to look back at this big disappointment with positive thankfulness, feeling that if she had had foreign instruction too early it might have impaired her still undeveloped individuality. An artist, always determined to follow her own path, she is able to say today of the European fiasco: "I think it has helped to keep my point of view in art. I was utterly unfit to meet on equal terms the various influences of modern art in Europe."

But if she could not go abroad, Wanda Gag could, and did, leave New York. Fashion plates might bring her money; they did not bring her joy; that much was clear. With what was left of her hard-earned savings she rented an old New Jersey farmhouse. She had been brought up a village girl; the pull of the country was strong. Besides, while still tight-shut in New York, she had been reading Thoreau's *Walden* and Knut Hamsun's *Growth of the Soil*, so she was feeling the call of quietness and of green spaces. Now, once and for all, she gave up commercial art. For years she had been drawing the human figure all dressed up in fashion-plate clothes. How much she must have hated doing this is proved by the fact that never since her declaration of independence has the "human form divine," except in a very few of her fairy-tale illustrations, appeared in any of Wanda Gag's pictures.

It was a dear, forlorn old place, that farm. She called it Tumble Acres. She rented it for seventy-five dollars the season, put in a little makeshift furniture, allowed herself thirty dollars a month for all expenses, and proceeded to live as she liked and paint what she pleased. She had three acres to be alone in. She both planted her own vegetables and painted them. Of her new freedom she writes, "I drew everything I saw, until I began to see beauty in the commonest things, from a radiator or a frying-pan to the living countryside. I did not try to draw for others as I had been doing. I sold practically nothing for years, but I began to find myself."

Today Wanda Gag's address is still an old farm within traveling distance of New York. And to New York she travels from time to time. She is known to the Children's Room of the New York Public Library. She is a small, vivacious person, in her first thirties, but looking as if she were in her first twenties. She is dark, short-haired, with a straight bang across the forehead, and beneath it quick, merry eyes and quick, merry lips. Her early hardships don't seem to have hurt her. She looks exactly as a child might expect the author of three of his favorite books to look. The books stand there on the shelves, very recent books, but delightful enough to be already well worn by eager small hands. Wanda Gag, highly imaginative eldest of a highly imaginative seven, of course had early practice in telling stories to children. Today she is telling them to a larger audience. Also in those far-off New Ulm days of her childhood she herself listened when the old transplanted Bohemian peasants told their folklore tales. In Wanda Gag's own tales today there are quaint reminders of earlier, Old World story-telling. The books, of course, are chiefly pictures, running up and down and across the words, which have their own magic, too. Kindly gnome-like little old men, stocky kindly little old women, homely cottage interiors, bring to mind all our associations with the Brothers Grimm. *Millions of Cats* is a slim, delicious volume first recounted to a group of child friends who clamored for a story. On its pages you really do seem to see millions of cats, actually acres of stalking feet and stuck-up tails. The artist made a business of living with two cats in order to draw her millions. The second animal book is all about *The Funny Thing*, who is not an animal at all, but

an horrific creature of Miss Gag's fancy, who has a
cruel habit of eating dolls, until, as the narrative
proceeds, he is persuaded to a diet of jumjills instead. *Snippy and Snappy* records the escapade of
two little field mice who wander too far from home.
One unforgettable page depicts the two petrified
with fear on a strange doorstep. The open door-
space looms high as the sky above them, and is absolutely black. Only two tiny field mice looking into a
limitless black unknown, but if one of us older ones
looks across some small reader's shoulder at that
illustration, we shall find ourselves suddenly becoming grave, just a little awed, perhaps. This is only a
child's picture book, but such a picture can evoke
even for an adult stark mystery. Wanda Gag is
herself at play when she makes her books for children, but even to them she is giving the best of her
inimitable art.

Wanda Gag, merely a Bohemian girl, child of
peasant immigrants, born and brought up in an iso-
lated village which under new skies continued the
Old World life; but a girl who has become one of
America's greatest artists, a girl who has always
felt something unique within her, and from the first
has been determined to let that something out. Today Wanda Gag's work is on permanent exhibition
in the Metropolitan Museum, New York, the British
Museum, London, the Art Institute, Chicago, and
in the Bibliothèque Nationale, Paris.

Wanda Gag's art is hard for anyone to describe,
for her choice of subjects and her treatment of them
is peculiarly her own. She seems able to charm both

the severe art critics and the humble members of the general public. Perhaps this is because all her work is so deeply human, and at the same time always a little whimsical. She does not draw the human figure, it is true, but she can make a bunch of carrots, a smoky lamp, a battered coffee-pot, human. Some one has said of her, "Contact with poverty has given her the power to interpret life, through common things, in a manner half ironic, half affectionate, but strangely moving." Something she herself has said of her work reveals the artist who is back of the pictures and the woman who is back of the artist. She is speaking of her delight in varied mediums, etchings, woodcuts, linoleum cuts, and last of all her experiment in painting on sandpaper. "Sandpaper," she says, "with its crystalline surface gives one scintillations, the quality of vibrations one so much wants, say in an interior which is perhaps a room some one has just gone out of." No admirer of her pictures has ever described the quality of them more truly than do these words of the artist herself. One recalls a black-and-white attic room by her hand. Near its window is a sagging old bedstead, human in its pathos, its weariness, its kindly welcome to some tired being who seems only just to have left. Wanda Gag has done many a black-and-white room now on exhibition in one great gallery or another, but every one of them is a room threadbare with poverty, and every one of them is a room strangely wistful, as if it were "a room some one has just gone out of."

Wanda Gag brought a great ability with her into

life, and out of life she has won another great ability. Today she stands unique among artists for her insight that can see beauty even in sordidness, and for her sure craftsmanship that can reveal that beauty to others.

CHAPTER II

PAMELA BIANCO,
FAMOUS SINCE SHE WAS TWELVE

IN AND OUT and about I twisted through the unfamiliar windings of Greenwich Village. At last I found the number given in the New York telephone directory under the name, "'Bianco, F." It was a drab, commonplace house. Looking at it, you would not have guessed the dreams flaming and dancing beneath its roof. I rang the bell of the topmost floor and the door jiggled open. I climbed dark stairs toward the voice and the face bending down to me from above. I gave at first only a passing handshake to Mrs. Bianco at the door, then I entered and said to the grave girl who took my hand, "So this is you!" She is now in her early twenties, but like many other people who have never seen her, I had known Pamela Bianco ever since she was fourteen, when somehow a magical book of pictures had floated to my humdrum desk.

I sat down and tried to say the usual things one says when one first meets people, things rarely recalled afterward. I tried to remember I had come for an interview; I attempted to keep in mind that, stranger though I was, Pamela Bianco and her mother probably expected me to be ordinarily courteous. I heard my voice talking, but I knew it wasn't saying anything, for the wall opposite to me, as I seated myself near the window, had taken my breath away. Out of the gray room a picture blazed into me, two young figures, life-size. Of course there could not be a red like that anywhere in the world except in an artist's brain—that rose-crimson of fairyland. Of course there could not be a gold like that anywhere except in a child's fancy—that silver-gold of fairyland. But, stupidly, I did not at first realize who alone could have painted that picture.

Most of us have forgotten how the world outside of us looked to us when we were two, or how the world inside of us looked to us when we were six. But Pamela Bianco has not forgotten. Nor has her mother. From her littlest childhood, Pamela has always been able to draw her dreams. And Mrs. Bianco has not forgotten how small children feel about their toys. Down at their publishers, people speak of *the* Biancos. Mother and daughter are one in their insight and approach, although the one employs a pen and the other a palette. Pamela knows that a three-year-old may see the unseeable, and so by means of pencil or brush she has been able to reveal to poor stodgy grown-ups the visions of a tiny child. And her mother knows what a three-year-old may feel about a toy, and so, in her books for children, she has been able to make toys alive even for dull-eyed adults, who would otherwise see only jointed wood or stuffed velveteen. When you see the name of Margery Williams Bianco attached to a volume, as for example, *The Little Wooden Doll,* or *The Velveteen Rabbit*, you may know at once that, no matter how old you are, in two pages you'll be under a spell such as only one author before has ever been able to weave. You will realize at once that Margery Williams Bianco is the direct descendant of Hans Christian Andersen. Sometimes there has been a rich combination of "the Biancos," when Pamela has illustrated her mother's books. She had not yet graduated from her own childhood when she made the pictures for *The Little Wooden Doll*. The pictures in her mother's book, *The Skin Horse*, are also hers.

I sat there remembering the magic of Mrs. Bianco's books, the elfin wizardry of Pamela's illustrations, and trying to realize that I was actually talking to the author and the artist. I knew, of course, that I should have been letting them do the talking, but, very quickly, I had realized that neither was particularly given to talking. Dreams I knew they must both always have in their heads, dancing, shining, incessant visions, but they don't, either of them, wear their dreams on their sleeves. I had the sensation that any older woman has, with many likable girls of today, that whether or not I, who had come to interview her, was getting Pamela Bianco, Pamela Bianco, all quietly, was getting me. She has a serious, silent face, which one comes to watch, delightedly, for the little come-and-go smile flitting across it. The unruffled blue eyes watching me were keen. It is my conviction and observation that no one who is big enough to be famous can ever be at the same time small enough to care. Pamela Bianco has been famous since she was a little girl—a dozen years or more. I think to be conscious of that fact would bore her beyond all bearing. Constantly, just back of her eyes she must be gazing at visions, visions such as are not seen by any other artist of our day. But this little fact does not prevent her being a most practical young person, quietly, competently, practical. There was not in that upper story any hint of "maid service." Pamela rose to serve us tea with a long-practiced hand. I think both she and her mother would be amused by my comment that Pamela is housewifely. Why shouldn't she be? Apparently they have always taken domesticity for granted. Why in the world should domesticity interfere with dreams? Of course one should remember that for three years Pamela Bianco has been a married woman, married to a young poet, Robert Schlick, of Portland, Oregon.

All the time that I was drinking tea, all the time that my tongue was conversing, I was slipping, slipping away into another world, an unearthly world that only a few earthly spirits are permitted to open to others. Dreamily I was entering that blazing, beautiful picture across from me there on the wall. There is not another object in that unobtrusive, homey room that I remember. I was beginning to ask myself, as I gazed, is it possible, possible? "Lemon? Sugar?" inquired my serious young hostess. And I gazing at that picture! Was it possible? Of course she had always done exquisite things. From the time she was five, Pamela Bianco has been able to insnare a beauty remote from earth. But this, there on the wall, was not only beauty; it was power.

Steadily, throughout that hour, I was trying to combine the Pamela Bianco I saw before me with that Pamela Bianco whose history I knew. Here was a girl of twenty-odd who not so many years ago was hailed all the world over as a child prodigy. Mentally I kept pondering, what made her a child prodigy in the first place, and then, what has kept her from being spoiled by her fame? For, clearly, she is a solidly sensible young person, although, inescapably, she must possess all the sensitiveness of the painter and the poet she actually is. Then there's a wide-spread opinion that a child genius, if it flowers too early, is rather likely to fade out later. If your talent lifts you to a well-deserved prominence when you're twelve, it's ten to one you'll not be heard of by the time you're twenty—or afterward. Before she was twelve Pamela Bianco had drawn the pictures that illustrate *Flora*, the book that brought to most of us our first knowledge of her. Today has her hand lost its fairy-given skill? Who painted that picture over there on the wall opposite my chair?

Of course Pamela Bianco started life under conditions extremely favorable for a child-artist. She began by selecting for herself a highly gifted pair of parents. Her mother, Margery Williams, is English to the bone, but she was born and educated in Philadelphia. She took to story-writing early, and published a novel when she was only eighteen. Then she went abroad, to live for a time in England, and to travel on the Continent. In Italy she met and married Captain Francisco Bianco. The other afternoon Mrs. Bianco assured me that "Captain" is a purely war-time decoration, which clings, though they make every effort to discard it. As a matter of fact there is nothing military about her husband; his

main interest was, is, and always has been, beautiful
books and beautiful book-making. In Italy the two
children were born, a son, who in 1930 graduated
from   Columbia   University,   New   York—and
Pamela. Her mother feels that Pamela's early developed ability is in part explained by transplanting.
A plant profits by being lifted from one flower-bed
to another, and in the same way little Pamela was
transplanted by circumstances, living and thriving
for a few years in one environment, then in another.
This kept her open-eyed and alert. I could not discover that the Biancos had any set theory of nursery
or post-nursery education, but they practiced a wise
and affectionate let-alone. They set out their seed-
lings in the best surroundings they could obtain, pro-
vided a setting of beauty and of books and of com-
radeship, and then they let them alone. As soon as
a small girl developed a very decided bent of her
own, they let that alone, too, most carefully, most
determinedly. When his children were small, the
father was often away. He used to offer them prizes
for producing a book to greet his return. Pamela did
her own illustrating. No intelligent parent, least of
all the Biancos, could have failed to recognize the
grace, the delicacy, the elfin charm, of Pamela's
drawings—there was a quality of magic even in the
guinea-pigs and fairies she drew when she was five.
Beyond all question the child possessed a talent
most rare and individual. Reverently her parents let
this talent grow in its own way. Pamela received no
art instruction whatever, and at eleven they took her
out of school that she might draw and paint her
head off if she wanted to. Sometimes she had tutors

and home instruction, as much as seemed positively necessary, and no more.

Before Pamela had reached her teens, the family had lived in Paris, then briefly in the United States, again in Paris, then in London, and later and longest in Italy, chiefly in Turin. In Turin, when Pamela was still a happy out-of-doors little girl, living in her drawing and her dreams, the Italian sculptor, Bistolfi, was moved to arrange an exhibition of children's art. Pamela's pictures were entered with the rest, but unlike the rest they were reproduced in Italian newspapers and magazines all over the country. "Not for a quarter of a century," writes Sherril Schell in the *Mentor* of December, 1924, "had an artist created such a stir in Italy as this thirteen-year-old girl." The greatest living poet of Italy, Gabriele d'Annunzio, spoke of Pamela Bianco, as "this wonderful child, whose name is like the name of a new flower. The drawings of the phenomenal girl artist are like flowers, delicate, fragile, windblown, sprung from the enchanted soil of fairyland."

A year later there was a transplanting of the household to London, and an exhibition which was to become known all around the world. Artists and poets, famous people of all sorts, titled ladies, royal personages, crowded the galleries. The Tate Gallery and the Kensington Museum purchased a little girl's pictures for their permanent collections. The English poet, Walter de la Mare, begged to write poems to fit Pamela's pictures. The result was that elf-made book called *Flora*, a book to be prized equally for the magic of its drawings and for the magic of the verses that accompany them.

The next change in Pamela Bianco's life was to New York, where she has spent her teens, and the first part of her still uncompleted twenties. The great London exhibition was followed by another in Manhattan, which was quite as enthusiastic as London over the girl artist. Since this, their last transplanting, the Biancos have settled comfortably into their spreading third floor above the twisty streets of Greenwich Village. The third floor includes the roof with its lounging-chairs and its sea breezes. Steadily Pamela has been painting, growing, trying new mediums.

Pamela Bianco has already done much. But she will do more. Her future is still before her—and before us. She is but just returned from the sojourn in Italy which followed her marriage in June, 1929. She has been traveling on a Guggenheim fellowship, and seeing Italy all over again for the first time since she was a little girl. But *what* has she seen, and what will she make us see? One thing promised us, I found out on inquiry, is *The Starlit Journey*, a book for children, her own words, the first to be printed, and her own illustrations. The title suggests the same unearthly magic that first appeared in *Flora*. But the chief promise lies in the fact that the author-artist herself describes the forthcoming volume as a book for children. It will therefore be a book that Pamela Bianco herself believes that children will love, and who in all the world today could know so well as she? As a child she was able to picture for us all the unbelievable loveliness of a child's fancies. This ability she has not lost, but she

sees deeper, farther, now into a child's soul, on its
lovely, lonely adventure. She has been in Italy, the
land that has given to the world its madonnas. There
could be only one source for the new depth and
power in Pamela Bianco's work. She has looked at
Italy's madonnas, she can now gaze into a child-
soul with a madonna insight. She has brought home
from Italy a madonna of her own. The picture has
not yet been put upon exhibition. But for an hour I
have sat looking at it, and I feel that Pamela Bianco
has done nothing like it, nothing so great, ever before. This her latest work recalls her earliest. It is
quite unlike the heavier, more decorative, plaques
and panels of her later teens. Inexplicably deepened
and intensified, "The Madonna of the Sailor" has
the very same qualities that Pamela Bianco revealed
when she was twelve—delicacy, magic, ethereal re-
moteness from earth. Life-size, the two figures, and
so young, both of them, the slim, kneeling mother,
and, standing, the white wisp of a naked child. The
two child-faces look straight ahead, in all their
strange, most delicate beauty. Their gaze is at something in a half-elfin world, at some mystery that
only Pamela Bianco can guess and with an enchanted
brush can suggest. The girl-mother's dress ripples
in folds of a burning, magic crimson. On the child's
breast flutters a tiny pennant, as if he stood on the
peak of some invisible ship with the winds of faëry
in its sails. The artist has conceived a child soul as
a mysterious, wee voyager, blown across a sea most
beautiful but most strange. It is a modern picture,
painted by a young artist of today, but perhaps it

possesses a timeless insight. "The Madonna of the Sailor"—perhaps that is an eternal name for a vision that has come to all madonnas once, as, looking into the future, they saw across strange waters the figure of a little child.

Chapter III

MARGUERITE KIRMSE, ETCHER OF DOGS

A FEW years ago the picture-shop windows broke out in an epidemic of Scotties. Even in the bookstore displays the delicious little impudent black dogs intruded. Their waggish pictures stood up against the grave piled volumes of philosophy and history. People pressed their noses against the plate glass staring at the antics of puppies. Customers who had come to purchase books were likely to find a puppy portrait quite irresistible and to march off with one in their pockets. Though that irruption of Scotties in the shop windows was rather sudden, it has not ceased. Twice a year the art dealers exhibit a new lot of them, just as whimsical as the others, and more so, for each year the etcher's hand achieves more cunning in reproducing to the life perky black ears, alert little noses, vibrant, small bodies, snappy, shoe-button eyes. Most of us know Marguerite Kirmse's Scotties, but few of us—and those are a lucky lot!—know Marguerite Kirmse herself.

One thing one could not help knowing about Marguerite Kirmse at the start. Seeing her pictures, every dog-lover recognizes a dog-lover. And one can guess even more about her than that, for no artist could catch the trick of a lifted paw, or the

23

twitch of an ear, as she does, who did not actually live with dogs and watch them from dawn to dark. You couldn't do that happily in the city, so one may make the further surmise that Marguerite Kirmse has her home in the country. She is one of the fortunate people who have reached the place where they can do the thing that makes them happiest and healthiest, and at the same time earn a living at it. In her busy out-of-door existence, Marguerite Kirmse must have difficulty in distinguishing between her work and her play, when both are so thoroughly enjoyable. That is one of the advantages gained by a woman who has given her life to dogs.

But a life given to dogs was not in her earliest program for herself, nor in her parents' earliest plans for their little girl. It often happens that a person is born with two overmastering tastes, and doesn't discover for many years which one is going to prove the stronger. Little Marguerite knew that she loved animals, but so did all her family, so that it did not occur to herself or to them that there was anything unusual in this. On the other hand, all of them loved music, so that when a small girl showed a bent in this direction, it was most natural that her education should be musical. Marguerite Kirmse was born at Bournemouth, England, where her parents conducted a successful private school. She had the typical English childhood, full of out-of-doors and full of animals. There was abundant time and room for little girls and for their pets—dogs, squirrels, rabbits, donkeys. There are school books still surviving from this early period, and down all the margins there is a capering procession of beasts, no space unscribbled. Here are dogs and horses from the familiar English countryside, and also lions and tigers from far-off imagined lands. But in that picture-gallery of school-book margins, there are always more dogs than any other animals. Child and woman, Marguerite Kirmse has always loved dogs best. There is more in them to love, she thinks.

But back there in Bournemouth in her first teens, nobody would have dreamed of making a career of dogs. So a musical mother taught the harp to a musical little daughter. It is rather strange, as one reads their lives, to discover how many women artists have first been musicians. There seems to be some underlying connection between the strokes of a brush or of a chisel and the hand-touch upon a musical instrument. Even this dog-lover girl, who was to become a portrait-painter of dogs, gave her first love to the harp. However, her delight in animals and her delight in music were still running a close competition inside of her when Marguerite Kirmse went up to London to complete her education. She was entered for study at the Royal Academy of Music, and at the same time, because of the ability she had already shown in animal sketches, she also took lessons at the School of Animal Painting. These lessons were not enough to satisfy her enthusiasm. In all free hours she was off to the zoo, studying the mechanism of an elephant's ear, the ripple of muscles in a panther's movements, the comic attitudes of a crane. For a while the strain of following two arts at once proved too much for a country girl's health. But the future career was not yet plain, for when forced to choose, she gave up her study of painting, but kept to her study of music.

When the student days were ended, the bread-and-butter problem began to intrude. Miss Kirmse now started making sketches for London papers and magazines, and also, her major talent now beginning to tug at her hand, she drew portraits of the winners at dog shows. None of this was very lucrative, however. Some friends about to start for New York made the suggestion that the weary young artist accompany them for change and rest. She went. Except for visits, Marguerite Kirmse has never returned to England. But at first there were some grim years, before, quite unexpectedly, her dogs were to make her fortune. Instead of dogs, she first turned to her harp. But with all its skill, her harp was not much wanted by the public. She earned a little money as harpist in a New Jersey church, but when an offer came to join an orchestra in Seattle, the membership fee in the musicians' union, one hundred dollars, was quite impossible. There were attempts at pictures, too, in oil, pastels, crayon. It was a discouraging stretch of life, it was almost despair, and then, suddenly, in came the dogs—and luck. For some time animals had been trying to nose their way back to Miss Kirmse's interest. The zoo in the Bronx had proved as attractive as the zoo in London, and the keepers had allowed the artist many privileges. But it was dogs, always dogs, who were most insistent to be in the pictures. Miss Kirmse began to make sketches of her friends' dogs, and to sell them. Then, one day, as she sat idle and dreamy, she picked up a phonograph needle. Somehow a piece of metal found itself in her other hand. The idle phonograph needle began to move, faster and faster, more and more gaily. And there on the metal was a wag of a dog—the first etching, and made before the artist had learned how to etch!

Her friends liked that first scratch of a dog as well as we like its many, many successors in the art dealers' windows today, and these friends sent the etcher-to-be to engravers and print dealers. Chief among these last was Arthur H. Harlow. When Miss Kirmse showed him her first crude attempts, his enthusiasm astonished her. It was the great beginning, and it was a dog that did it. Nowadays twice a year there are half a dozen new etchings, and a limited edition of copies. The plates of these are then destroyed, and each copy becomes correspondingly precious. A single little etching may today bring as much as seven hundred and fifty dollars.

But money is the least part of the luck that dogs have brought to Miss Kirmse. They have also bestowed a husband and a farm, a home for herself and unnumbered homes for her canine friends. The name of the first is George W. Cole; the name of the second is Arcady Farm; and the name of the last is Tobermoy Kennels. Today Marguerite Kirmse Cole is not only an etcher of dogs, but a breeder. She is probably much prouder of the blue ribbons awarded to the dogs she has raised than of the name and fame awarded to the dogs she has etched. Privileged people who know Arcady Farm tell us it is as happy a place as its name implies. It is in the foothills of the Berkshires, near Bridgewater, Connecticut. Overlooking the Housatonic Valley, a hundred and fifty green acres roll away in comfortable seclusion, yet still within easy reach of New York. The farm runs along a ridge and has a view of mountains as well as of lowland. The surrounding country is a gentle bit of old New England, with quiet farmhouses and fencerows of mossy stone. At the highest point of the ridge there used to be an old tobaccobarn, now converted into a delightful farmhouse, all white with apple-green trimmings. Gentle elm trees throw flickering shadows over the jutting front doorway, we are told. At the back a rockery is piled right up to the piazza rail, all a gay mass of flowers, with the roof of the well-house rising in the midst of the blossoms, a well-house from which comes the purest of water. Everywhere one sees the Sign of the Scottie, trade-mark, and home-mark, too. There is a Scottie stenciled on the rural mail-box.

The doors of Arcady farmhouse welcome you straight into the living-room. It is a house planned by the owners, and it is a lived-in home. The Coles have done much of the work of it with their own hands. The big solid dining-table is witness to Mr. Cole's expert carpentry. Both living-room and dining-room have jolly big fireplaces of native stone. The beams of the original barn stretch across the ceilings. The living-room runs the height of two stories, and around the second extends a musicians' balcony. There at times the artist mistress of the house becomes also a minstrel. The harp that belonged to her English girlhood stands there in the gallery of her New England home, and many visitors have enjoyed her playing. Three guest-rooms

with their green-leaved windows attest the hospital-
ity of Arcady Farm.

Another dilapidated farmhouse has been restored
to service as a summer studio. Visitors tell us it is
a pleasant green walk's distance from the main
house and holds all the tools and equipment both
for etching and for painting. But by no means all
the artist's time is spent in her studio. The farm
and the flowers, and above all the dogs, have a claim
upon all the hours of the master and the mistress of
Arcady. Both of them are up at five-thirty, and busy
about the place. The dogs are up even earlier, and
they are busy, too.

You would never dream that any one woman
could love so many, many dogs. Every guest is in-
troduced to a raft of puppies. Every guest is also
led to converse with a group of serious older canines.
Most of the dogs are Scotties, since producing Scottie pups is the chief object of Tobermoy Kennels,
but there are other dogs, too—an occasional aire-
dale or such a beautiful pointer as stalks noiselessly
through the tall grass in one of Miss Kirmse's latest
etchings, called "Point". You soon discover that
Marguerite Kirmse is no ordinary dog-lover, but
the kind of person to whom every dog is also a
person. She is out to discover individuality in every
fresh litter. Before a pup has its eyes open, while
it is still only a nuzzling bit of sooty black, Miss
Kirmse will have detected some special trait of
character that reminds her of some worthy ancestor
deceased or sold to strange hands. Real children
could hardly be more tenderly and patiently trained

in good manners than are the hobbledehoy pups of
Arcady Farm. Love and a sense of humor form
the key to the educational methods of this mistress-
teacher. As a visitor listens while she presents one
wriggling little black personage after another, he
may wonder how she ever manages to sell any of
these well-loved friends. Of course every dog you
meet at Arcady Farm has a name and a history, and
also probably a future. There is Nora, who out of
a long-forgotten dreary stretch of homesickness has
developed an undying devotion. There is Mickey,
an Irish terrier, eager, imaginative, highly tempera-
mental. Sometimes a name once bestowed has to be
changed later to fit changed circumstances—as in
the case of a dainty dark lady once called Lady
Babby, because she recalled the witchery of Barrie's
heroine in *The Little Minister*. But Lady Babby
was lent to a friend of the family's for a visit, during which she was so stuffed with food that she returned quite unrecognizable, and because of her
resemblance to a certain dumpy type of airship was
rechristened Black Blimpo. Some canine dwellers in
Arcady have left the imprint of their personality
upon the place long after their deaths. The Coles
still speak with a deep, remembering affection of
Heath, that wise, devoted little mother of many
litters, from which today survive three strong, sooty
sons, Big Boy, Heath, and Midget.

We people who cherish a Kirmse etching, we people who think that we are pretty good ourselves at
loving our dogs, need to listen to some words spoken
at Tobermoy Kennels, by one who has mastered not

only the art of etching dogs, but the art of loving them: "If dogs could talk I often wonder how high some of us would rate in canine esteem. I am afraid I know only too well how low some of us would fall, for all too many dog-owners seem to take their dog's affection so much for granted that they forget to ask themselves if they are doing their part in upholding an undying friendship and in retaining a loyalty born of love."

Because dogs swarm over her in happy outdoor freedom all day long, the artist has a chance to catch her models in all their swift unconscious poses, a guzzling puppy, a dignified mother, a graceful hunter motionless while he points to a covey of partridges. Ideas for etchings are always dancing through Miss Kirmse's mind. Perhaps a study for a picture occurs to her in a crowded subway or department store, though of course her pictures come to her oftenest on her happy New England farm. She keeps pad and pencil always ready to catch some puppy's whimsical antics, and she has pad and pencil also handy for any fancy that may come to her at night. Her puppy pictures never become stale. It is Mrs. Cole who sees the whimsicalities of the pups and somehow fastens them, all wriggling and alive, on paper, but it is Mr. Cole who names the pictures. "Let's Eat" presents a small Scottie all alone in a large tin pan, wherein he appears to have licked up every crumb. "Safety First" shows two tense eager blackies, facing each other across the bone that lies between them on the flagstone walk, while, peeping with equal caution, from the half-opened door is still a third little black friend with designs upon that bone. "Your Letter Received," exhibits the tiniest of Irish terriers, wearing an air of studied detachment from the torn missive before him. Mr. Cole not only supplies titles for the pictures, but he is his wife's agent in all the business details of her picture-making.

Marguerite Kirmse has a studio in New York as well as in Connecticut. It is full of Scottie mementos, and sometimes an actual Scottie comes down from his hills for a city visit. There is a Scottie on the cigarette boxes, a Scottie on the radiator of the automobile. On the letter from Miss Kirmse near my hand as I write these words, there is at the lower left-hand corner a Scottie seated, with inquiring nose upturned toward the spider swinging from the web at the upper right.

There in her mid-town studio, which somehow manages to reflect some of the happy, outdoor sunshine of Arcady Farm, Marguerite Kirmse not only makes etchings of dogs, but also paints portraits of blue-ribbon canine notables, just as she did in her earlier, harder days. She is still today not greatly changed in spirit from the little English girl who raced with her dogs about that old Bournemouth home across the Atlantic. In our new world she has found deep satisfaction, and says so. She is a woman profoundly happy in her work, but also wise enough to realize that all good work requires its hours of relaxation and forgetting. She is all for seeking first the work you want, and then doing it with a will. "All the good work in the world won't

give you satisfactory results," she is quoted as saying, "unless you enjoy what you are doing. I love my
work and I have never had too much of it, but I do
have to guard against overwork. In any creative
job there is danger of going stale."

CHAPTER IV

MARGARET BOURKE-WHITE,
PHOTOGRAPHER OF STEEL

You must climb to meet her. You must mount exactly sixty-one stories above midtown New York in
order to see her. Even then you may wait two hours,
as I did, before you really do see her except in darting flashes. The Chrysler Tower, with its needle
point pricking the sky, is two years old. Its photographer is twenty-six, and she has risen to her present
eminence as rapidly as did the tower, and, as I was
presently to discover, on quite as sure foundations.
Margaret Bourke-White is the leading industrial
photographer of the world, and for this fact there
are good reasons, some of which I observed for
myself, some of which she told me.

Margaret Bourke-White has photographed darting flame. I wonder what kind of camera would be
required to photograph the darting flame she is herself. In her sky-high studio I waited and watched
and listened. It was in no sense a hectic spot, but it
fairly crackled with energy. Yet, up there among the
clouds, it had a calm like the center of a rapid wheel.
Perhaps the quietly competent English secretary,
Mrs. Fraykin, had something to do with this. The
telephone kept demanding interviews and having to
be politely pacified. Packets of photographs were

34

arriving and leaving. Doors would open into mysterious interiors, and emit keen-faced photographer-men holding dripping plates. They seemed to be a young and genial sort, appearing to enjoy the hustle. Important-looking gentlemen entered and were closeted with the slim, quick-moving chief. And sometimes the chief herself flashed through and gave a terse direction—a dominating person, though brief-spoken. When the gray tailored coat of her suit was swung off, there was brilliance beneath the gray, a dash of cerise lighting up a small dark face. Flying past me, she would speak a swift word of apology for my delay. I imagined there were moments when Margaret Bourke-White might have appeared merely a charming, brown-hued slip of a girl nearer sixteen than twenty-six. But there was a keenness in those dark eyes that made me feel she was abundantly worth waiting for, even if the minutes did keep slipping around the clock-face.

It was a live place in which to wait. Entrance room and office and balcony, and, most of all, the studio itself, were interesting, every wall and window of them. Everywhere there were Russian posters, bold and black and red. On her two visits, Russia has offered Margaret Bourke-White much besides its posters; in fact, everything she might ask, for she entered with a pack of photographs under her arm, photographs having a stark, unbelievable new beauty, revealing the new glory and power of machinery. Rightly or wrongly, today Russia regards the machine as its god of deliverance. So Russia has twice given Margaret Bourke-White a most sincere welcome, and unlimited official assistance, as she has traveled everywhere, taking pictures of Russia in action.

I was prepared to find Russia in the Bourke-White studio, but I wasn't prepared to find reptiles. The reptiles are not a fad, but, as I was to find out, quite as lively an interest as Russia for this many-sided young person. On the parapeted balcony swung above the infinitesimal city streets deep below, three tortoises keep up a sluggish parade. In an aquarium just within the door there's a small and recent alligator, guarded by the notice,

"Cleaners!
    Please take care. Do *not* move this alligator. Thanks."

Once admitted to the inner studio and left alone there, I didn't really care how long I had to wait. It is an indescribable sort of place, yet it makes you long to describe it. It is modernistic, the work of John Vassos. It is triangular, but you don't at first perceive the triangle because of the unobtrusive juttings and recesses. The general effect is of light rather than of color, yet when you look you will discern the unobtrusive rose, the unobtrusive buff. There is indirect lighting so concealed you have to look for its source, and the chief impression I got was silver—silver twilight deepening into dusk. The aquarium catches the eye first and holds it longest. It is placed so high against the wall that a miniature set of steps and a balcony are needed to reach it. The block of seeming ice within, and the green aquatic plants, give forth a glow half bewitched, silver and emerald. Goldfish float in the

water and funny little black fish, looking like flap-
ping bits of charred tissue paper.

But the windows are the life of the studio, looking
three ways. I stepped softly from one to the other.
It was quite plain from here that Manhattan is an
island. I could see its far tip and its two rivers, wind-
ing, a dull silver, in and about its toy streets, its
pygmy skyscrapers. It was an evening of such rolling clouds as Margaret Bourke-White loves to
photograph as background for some ink-black
smokestack. Behind the cloud-bank on my right the
sun was sinking, in a subdued, half-seen glow, much
like the indirect lighting within the studio. Alone up
there, I kept thinking of this strange beautiful setting for a most up-to-date and thriving industry,
Margaret Bourke-White's enterprise. In old times
people used to go down to the sea in ships and do
their business in the great waters. Nowadays they
go up to the sky and do their business among the
clouds. It seems to me this high location should have
some effect on the business itself, making it soar
above mere money-making. But does it? The answer
is Margaret Bourke-White's photography—and
Margaret Bourke-White herself.

A million pin points of lights were pricking the
dusky city stretched like a map below me. Other
people were all gone at last, the photographer-men,
the visitors, the secretary, even the tortoises had
been put to bed, and even the telephone was still.
The Chrysler Tower, just now humming with business, was deserted except for Margaret Bourke-
White and me in the soft-lit studio. A slim, taut
body, clad in dusky gray and cerise, relaxed against

the couch cushions. Perhaps she was too tired to talk to me? Not a bit, for I had asked her to talk of a subject she loves. At twenty-six she has climbed to be one of the most eminent photographer-artists of the world. Not so long ago she was poverty-poor and obscure. Today, so states the periodical, *Time,* she earns a yearly income of $50,000. "But what of the years before all this?" I inquired of her. "Tell me about your little-girlhood. What inheritance accounts for the sharpness of your vision? Who and what taught you the sure fire of your camera? Who, what, first led you to perceive the stark grandeur of a glowing blast furnace?" And where, I wondered, had she learned that painstaking which, as I heard, makes her sometimes destroy a thousand films before being satisfied with one.

It was worth while listening to Margaret Bourke-White's story of herself, because that story, as she told it, was so little about herself, and so much about her parents. There is artist blood in her heritage. A great-uncle was the architect of many of the public buildings in Dublin. But her father is the chief reason for all that Margaret Bourke-White has become. He died nine years ago, but he became alive for me while his daughter spoke of him. He was an inventor, directing his efforts to perfecting printing processes, and himself inventing the color press. What chiefly impressed his daughter was his power of concentration. As a tiny girl she would watch him sitting silent for hours, thinking so hard that he seemed completely unconscious of all that was going on about him. The idea for some invention would come to him sometimes just as he woke up from

sleep. His wife always kept a pad ready to his hand
at night. He taught his three children chess, trying
to make them visualize five moves back or forward.
He himself could visualize the moves of an entire
game. He was a nature-lover, too. He and his little
Margaret had unforgettable walks. He could bring
a bird to him with his whistling. He showed the
child the paths of the stars. He took up tortoises and
snakes in his hands. One summer the little girl
watched the ways of two hundred caterpillars in her
keeping. Another summer the place was overrun
with her baby snakes.

Out of those early years with her father Margaret Bourke-White remembers many things. When
she was only eight she held her father's hand as,
spellbound, she watched the glowing ore of a smelt-
ing furnace. There are other aspects of her father's
influence still strong upon her. "I can never forget
how he loved truth!" she says. And she can never
forget how his work-people loved him. Because of
his connection with the Hall Printing Press Com-
pany in their home town of Bound Brook, New
Jersey, he came to know the factory people so well
that once he was the only person who could plead
with them during a strike. When he was stricken
with paralysis, the men begged to carry him about
the plant in a chair.

About her mother, too, still living and active, the
daughter speaks in glowing terms. Mrs. Bourke-
White, taking up life afresh in her widowhood, is
absorbed in work for the blind at Perkins Institute,
Boston. There is no blind person there who doesn't
have instant news of Margaret Bourke-White's

mounting achievements. They have all listened to
every word of her book, *Eyes on Russia*. The
mother has always had a keen interest in science.
On a shelf in the studio is a set of Huxley purchased
by her when a girl. For various qualities of her own
Margaret Bourke-White thanks her parents' example and training. Today she is as famous for her
fearlessness as for her photography. With her precious camera she scales scaffolding as carelessly as
a steeplejack. "My mother taught me not to be
afraid of anything," she says, and she sums up an
hour of tribute, "Both my parents always put things
through. They always dug things out for themselves."

The home background has been the foundation
for a mounting career which has been quite as
dogged and painstaking as it has been spectacular.
Luckily, Margaret Bourke-White is as much a business woman as she is artist and photographer. And
she has needed to be, for, left poor at her father's
death when she was seventeen, she had to struggle
hard for an education. With her varied tastes, she
didn't at first know what she wanted to be. There
was within her the pull both of artist and of naturalist. Her high-school years at Plainfield, New Jersey,
were followed by a year at Columbia. The art side
of her took a course at the Clarence H. White
School of Photography, and the naturalist side of
her sometimes carried her pet snakes with her to
classes. Next, her interest in reptiles swept her off
to two years at the University of Michigan, which
offered an excellent course in herpetology. But the
Michigan period was cut short for lack of funds,

and the girl came to Cleveland, where her family were now living, and took a position for a year in the Cleveland Museum of Natural History. The next move was to Cornell, where in 1927 she received her A.B.

At Cornell her future career began to clear before her. She took photographs of building and campus, and organized a group of students to sell them on commission. The sale soon eased the poverty problem. The pictures won such popularity that in Easter vacation the girl photographer carried a portfolio of them to New York to show them to architects there. She met enthusiasm everywhere, and orders and purchasers. From that spring of 1927 on, her fortune and her fame have steadily increased, but not yet was the direction of her ability quite determined. She had photographed landscapes and public buildings; she had not yet become supremely the artist of steel. She had not yet climbed to the high point of the Chrysler Tower to photograph it before it was complete, hanging there unsupported, a thousand feet in air, though it required three men to hold her camera against the icy wind.

A return to Cleveland was finally to reveal to Margaret Bourke-White the chief interest of her life. She wandered about the Cleveland "Flats," observing and photographing industry in the raw—smokestacks, and mills, and furnaces. She was fascinated by getting on paper the spirals of smoke, the pouring of molten ore. Her pictures came to the attention of the publicity chief of one of the Cleveland banks, and promptly they became a uniquely beautiful booklet, *The Romance of Steel,* sent to all depositors and to all bank executives all over the country. Meanwhile, this girl just from college was photographing the great estates along the lake. One of these estates belonged to the president of the Otis Steel Mill. The young photographer begged a favor. Might she photograph the mill in all its aspects? The permission given, the great man was off to Europe for five months. When he returned he received twelve pictures selected from a thousand discarded during five months of dogged effort after perfection. But the perfection of these twelve pictures has meant invitations to photograph all the great industries in the United States, in Canada, in Germany, and lately in Russia.

In 1929 the *Fortune* magazine brought Miss Bourke-White to New York and made her one of its editorial staff, a position she still holds, although most of her time has to be devoted to the ever-increasing business of her own studio. In the summer of 1930 the magazine sent her to take pictures of the great industries of Germany, and, quite on her own, she slipped off for six weeks in Russia. Her introduction was her portfolio. After seeing it the Soviet authorities gave her the run of the country. She went everywhere with official approval and at government expense. In September, 1931, she went again, traveling this time chiefly by airplane. The result of her first trip was a marvelously illustrated book, *Eyes on Russia,* her own photographs accompanied by her own account. And that account shows that the author can use words quite as skillfully as she can use a lens. A camera reveals but makes no comment. Neither does Margaret Bourke-

White. Her eyes, like the eyes of the camera, looking at Russia, see surfaces but do not claim to see below surfaces. Yet both her lens that reveals and her words that record, flash before the reader of her book thoughts that penetrate the surface. Margaret Bourke-White does not announce that there is stark grinding deprivation in Russia; she merely gives a detail, inexorable as the line of light on one smokestack in one of her pictures, by narrating that when the black cloth used to cover her camera box blew far away in the high wind, she was not able in all Russia to obtain another yard of black material. She does not use a page to tell us that Russian women are starving for pretty clothes; she merely mentions, with no more elaboration than her camera would employ, that the devoted interpreter-girl who accompanied her everywhere, begged for the metal ring fastening a can of cheese and wore it ever after as a bracelet.

Miss Bourke-White's second trip to Russia, in the fall of 1931, has resulted in a series of articles in the *New York Times* of the spring of 1932. She found Russia still charging ahead with its Five-year Plan, which on her first journey she had described "as a great scenic drama unrolled before the eyes of the world." One hopes that these, her second impressions of Russia, will eventually form a book like the first. More than her first account these articles reveal the men and women and children back of the vast, on-moving machines. The writer shows a great understanding, a great sympathy, with an alien people. Her pictures reveal Margaret Bourke-White as a photographer quite as much interested

in faces as in the nation's tractors that roll across
the limitless fields, or the gaunt mounting bridge-
heads above a vast seething river. In these pictures
those far-off Russians, so puzzling to our Western
comprehension, look out at us alive and near—
heavy peasant faces, some of them, with an age-old
patience written upon them, and with these the
quick faces of young men and girls, smiling, likable.
But best of all and most enlightening are the faces
of the Russian children that Margaret Bourke-
White's camera has brought home to us. There they
sit, avid and alive, in the rough-hewn school-room,
keen, eager, healthy faces—boys and girls, as the
camera shows them, who must inevitably bring new
things to pass in an old world. A new Russia has
been lucky in having a new-world photographer to
capture and reveal its dreams.

Margaret Bourke-White is an all-of-a-piece person. With her whole being she responds to all that
she sees everywhere around her. And what she sees
is a new world quivering with light and shade and
color, throbbing with all the pushing energy of the
machine, not yet to be calculated, only to be photographed. She does not presume to say how high our
skyscrapers may yet climb, how far our bridge spans
may yet swing, what yields our monstrous tractors
may yet achieve. What interests her is not prophecy,
but photography. In Russia as in America she is
absorbed in making pictures of an industrial giant
as he moves, as he rises. The more accurate her pictures, so she feels, the truer will be their record of
history. That is what drove her and her camera to

Russia, the impulse to perceive and to catch the swift history of an unprecedented experiment.

It is always a gripping experience to listen while an artist speaks of his art. High in the shadowy Chrysler Tower that evening, I listened while a new artist spoke of a new art. To every age its own manifestation of energy, she said, and always some new form of artistic response peculiarly fitted to interpret this new energy. To the Egyptians their pyramids, to the Athenian his Parthenon, to the Renaissance its painting, to us of today the machine. But we have not realized the beauty of the machine, its stark soaring lines, its massed bridge piers, its furnaces glowing in the dark with streaming molten ore. The power and the beauty and the sublimity of the machine require a new expression. Photography, therefore, becomes the art best interpretative of this period. But as I listened to a voice that seemed all aglow with dreams, I thought to myself, but it must be photography directed by an artist's vision and perfected by an artist's infinite painstaking.

It was quite dark when I stepped out from the long, long elevator shaft to the roaring, seething street. High up there in the studio above the clouds it had been very still, and I had done some far thinking, thinking elusive to capture and to compress into a portrait. Margaret Bourke-White can catch the leap of flame and make it alive in a photograph, but no interviewer can catch and make alive on the printed page that leaping flame she is herself.

CHAPTER V

META WARRICK FULLER,
LEADING SCULPTOR OF HER RACE

WITHIN the last quarter-century we have become accustomed to welcoming to high place Negro artists of great ability. Quietly and unassumingly Mrs. Meta Warrick Fuller has slipped into her position as leading sculptor of her race. Today the wife of a famous Negro nerve specialist, she has long since won an acknowledged greatness, but so unobtrusively that it is easy to believe that all her life she has felt it more important to be a person than to be an artist. Being a person has meant for her, successively, being a devoted daughter, a devoted wife, a devoted mother. Being a person means also for her, today, having a deeply interested share in all the activities of her New England community.

Meta Warrick was born of a line of educated colored people. For more than a century Philadelphia has possessed a group of colored citizens living quietly and conservatively, intent on the values of a happy family life, and of beauty as they found it in out-of-doors, in art, and in books. Not much heard of, these people, and not desiring to be, yet making a fine, unnoted contribution to the life of their city and of their nation. When Garrison, the great New England abolitionist, was struggling to start his paper, the *Liberator*, a Philadelphia Negro was the first man to send him money.

It was into a humble but serene home setting, where high, old-fashioned standards of living were maintained, that little Meta Warrick was born in June, 1877. She remembers herself as a highly sensitive and excitable child, but seems, even when very small, to have had almost too much ability to keep her feelings concealed. A devoted family were often totally unaware of hurts the little girl had suffered until she suddenly broke into wild crying or became actually ill. She recollects still the agony of a disappointment when she was only five. The possibility of a picnic party of little friends had been casually discussed, and then completely forgotten by the grown-ups. All in silence little Meta had counted the days, the hours, the minutes. The last minute arrived, and no picnic! She shut herself in a closet and cried so long and loud that her uncle next door came in to know the trouble. After that a considerate family guarded her from all disappointment so carefully that they never so much as mentioned any happy event in prospect until the actual hour had come.

Meta was a delicate little girl and, being much younger than her brother and sister, was much alone. Like many gifted children, she showed herself dull and shy in school, but in her solitary games her imagination ran riot. She built an elfin grotto in the city back yard. A single syringa bush made a magic woodland for herself and a tiny china doll. A garden hose supplied a glinting fountain. The little girl would sit for hours with a picture book, conversing with the characters on every page. She was especially fond of music; she would lie hidden and motionless under the piano while her sister played, would listen wide-eyed in her bed when neighbors came in to sing in the evening, and afterwards would repeat the tunes correctly enough, while making her own fantastic versions of words she could not understand. All by herself she loved to sit and touch the piano keys, and then talk to the little people she was sure she had waked, far inside at the end of the strings. Very sensitive she was to the sights as well as to the sounds all about her. At some unremembered date when she was still very small she was taken to Boston on the Fall River boat. The waking before dawn, to watch the shadowy figures and the bobbing lanterns of the deck hands is for her a picture still as vivid as any painting she was to see later in the galleries of Paris.

Meta Warrick's childhood was all alight with imagination; she saw fairy people and she heard fairy music. Most luckily for a youngster who lived so completely in an unreal world, there was a very real and devoted father always there to watch and guard and to sympathize with every shining fancy. Her very happiest childhood memory is of that father's companionship. When Meta was still small enough to beg to be carried when she was tired, her father would take her walking in Fairmount Park. All her joy in green meadows and green trees and twining water dates back to those long ago walks with her father.

Meta's fancies did not reveal the definite line her artistic nature was to take until her older sister be-

gan to have art lessons in the public school. At the
first sight of the sketches brought home, and of the
bits of clay, the little sister's unsuspected talent
kindled and flamed. In a year or two Meta was herself receiving the coveted art instruction, but at first
on only one day of the week. In the top floor of the
building where she went to school was located the
Tadd School of Industrial Art. Here once a week a
magic door was opened to the school children of
the floors below, and they received training in drawing, designing, modeling, and wood-carving. This
opportunity was an educational experiment on the
part of the authorities, and of it Mrs. Fuller writes
today, looking back, with deepest appreciation, saying of that priceless one day a week, that it "has
developed some of our present-day artists and architects, for here real talent was discovered and allowed to develop." For another opportunity of
these schoolgirl years Mrs. Fuller is even more
grateful, for in retrospect she recalls that "this was
the period during which my father took me to art
exhibitions and together we lived in the pictures we
saw, and the sculpture overwhelmed us." The two
comrades did not confine their shared joys to visits
to the wide, green park, nor to the spellbinding art-
galleries, they had the theater, too. Meta Warrick's
early pleasure in seeing plays may be divined from
the highly dramatic quality of the statuettes she was
to model later in Paris. But Paris was not yet a
name even for one's farthest dreams. It was quite
enough for Meta's delight, at this early stage of her
career, that she was seeing and hearing "Pinafore"
and "Patience" for the first time.

The Tadd School of Art was not only making the experiment of giving the children of the public schools a day a week of its teaching; it was following up this experiment by offering a year's scholarship to the most promising pupil thus discovered. It was but natural that Meta Warrick should win such a scholarship and should continue to have for three years afterward all the advantages of the best art instruction her native city could give her. It was in these years of absorbing study that the idea of Paris began to shape in her mind. The principal of the art school was insistent that so gifted a pupil should travel on to the greatest of all art centers. Shy and inexperienced as she was, Meta, at seventeen, sailed off one September day for the famous unknown city of her dreams.

Life was not to be easy in Paris, nor was the young girl to find friends at first. Gently protected all her life as she had been, she was probably not prepared for her first rebuff. Meta Warrick's picture at this date reveals her as very pretty, slight, small, and not very dark. In making her application for a cheap room at the American Girls' Club, Meta had not mentioned her color, but on her arrival at the Club, tired and breakfastless, the secretary mentioned it! The American Girls' Club was for white girls only! It seemed a big city to discover a home in, for a little dark-skinned stranger, now for the first time quite on her own. Hunger for art, however, was stronger than homesickness, and Meta Warrick, quiet as she was, was dogged. She meant to stay in Paris, and she did, finding a studio to sublet, and presently making friends with fellow-students, both white and colored, with French and English.

It wasn't at first all that she had expected, that dreamed-of sojourn in Paris. Meta studied drawing with Collin. She attended lectures on anatomy at the Ecole des Beaux-Arts. In the second year of her stay she went back to her loved modeling, a pupil at Colarossi's. Meanwhile she was steadily acquiring knowledge of French. She was meeting, in her own studio or theirs, Negro students, Negro artists. Chief among the latter was Henry Tanner, the famous Negro painter. At the Paris Exposition of 1899 there was a special exhibition of Negro achievement in the United States. This exhibition brought many of Meta's race to the city, and some of them discovered a friendly welcome in the girl artist's studio home.

Before she left Philadelphia Meta had promised her family to return in two years, but the two years had only showed her the length and the toil of any artist's climb to accomplishment. Her plea for more time in Paris won a third year, and in that year things began to happen. Meta had been an unwearied worker at her clay, and her clever fingers had done things the Paris critics were discovering. Quiet, retiring girl as she was, something of her childhood imagination broke loose when Meta Warrick touched clay. She delighted in making little models not a foot high, but she could put a whole life's terror or despair or longing into these few inches of clay. One of these little figures was of Œdipus when he had put out his own eyes; another, more grewsome still, was called, "A Man Eating

His Heart." Still far from satisfied with her Parisian adventure, the young artist at last nerved herself for an encounter. She grasped her statuette of the "Man Eating His Heart," and with it one day she went bravely to the greatest sculptor of all in Paris, Rodin. The great man received the small artist, he received into his hand the small statue. But he did not speak. For minute after minute he did not speak. The waiting girl knew he was not supposed to take any pupils. But within half an hour he had taken her! He offered to criticize anything she could bring, and more, he offered to come to her if her statues should ever become too cumbersome to carry!

Now with Rodin's praise to help her, Meta Warrick had her first taste of fame. The critics hailed the daring originality of her little figures, so tiny, yet so full of a strange power. Dealers began to seek her, purchasers appeared. Just a little more, just a little longer, and her growing reputation might have become world-wide. But just now, just here, Meta Warrick packed her trunk and went home. Why? Because to her, home was home and her three years were up. After all, when it came to a choice, she preferred to be a person, a daughter, first, an artist afterward.

But making an artist's way was even harder in Philadelphia than in Paris. Her native city did not want native art. The girl's imagination was seething with new creations, but no dealer would consider them—no domestic art, they said; importations only. But Meta Warrick worked on doggedly in her Philadelphia studio, and in 1907 was successful in securing one important commission. She made for the Jamestown Exhibition of this year fifteen groups of figures, in historic costume, showing the life of the Negroes in the three hundred years of the Virginia Colony.

In 1909 once more the person inside her seemed to her more important than the artist, and Meta Warrick married Dr. Solomon C. Fuller, of Framingham, Massachusetts. Dr. Fuller is a native of Liberia, and was educated there and in North Carolina. A neurologist at the Massachusetts state insane asylum at the time of his marriage, he has continued to build up a noteworthy practice and reputation. His Philadelphia bride promptly became absorbed in all the happy domesticity of a delightful home in a Boston suburb. In the years that followed, her art was to be crowded out, or at least postponed, by the interests of three lively little sons. All the old pushing impulse to make clay stand up and move and feel was still further checked by an unexpected disaster. All the equipment of the Philadelphia studio, which had been left in storage, was completely destroyed by fire. Despair at this unforeseen calamity drove the young mother for a time to throw herself more whole-heartedly than ever into the happy but engrossing daily tasks of home. But her artist reputation found her out in spite of her withdrawal. In 1913 Burghardt Du Bois, Negro leader and editor of the *Crisis*, sent a letter of appeal. The Negroes of New York were about to celebrate the anniversary of Emancipation. Dr. Du Bois himself was the author of a pageant to be given on successive nights. An exhibition of Negro achievement would be on display. Would not the chief sculptor of her race send a statue that might fittingly represent the spirit of Emancipation?

This appeal won. The housekeeping was shoved aside while tools were purchased and a space of cellar transformed into a studio. There Mrs. Fuller modeled a group—no longer tiny and fanciful, but strong and great—which revealed her own conception of the Negro becoming aware of his freedom. A photograph of this group is under my eyes as I write. It reveals a change within the sculptor since the days of those weirdly powerful statuettes that seemed to be the natural expression of the girlhood days in Paris. There is power in these two tall figures, but it is not now the power of intense emotion, it is the power of quiet expectation. Slim, straight, nearly nude figures they are, a Negro boy and girl, their backs against a great unshaped tree trunk, their faces gazing in steadfast confidence into some unknown future. One other figure there is, a kneeling woman behind the boy, a woman whose arm is lifted to shield her eyes from some deep wrong. Mrs. Fuller's own name for this group fresh from her imagination is "Humanity Freeing the Slave Youth and Maiden."

Although she does not confine herself to depicting her own people, more and more Mrs. Fuller seems concerned with the problems of her race. Or perhaps, if one judges her present work with true intuition, it might be more accurately said that she is more and more concentrated not so much on the problems of her race, as on its dreams and hopes and its sure developing capacities. This aspect of her

own convictions is shown in one of her statues now
in the Harlem library in New York. It is a figure
that seems to symbolize power as it wakes up to its
own possibilities, this straight, almost Egyptian,
young colored girl, passive as yet, but about to move
with swift, straight steps—to some place new and
high. Again Mrs. Fuller's name for this statue reveals her own high confidence in her people's future,
for she calls it "Ethiopia Awakening."

The Meta Warrick Fuller of today shares very
happily and completely the life of her community.
While her early love of sculpture seems to be re-
asserting itself in fresh and beautiful ways, she still
finds time to be a person in those ways demanded
of every public-spirited woman in every town. That
enlightening reference book, *Who's Who in Colored
America,* under Mrs. Fuller's name, gives a list of
activities, suggesting to any woman's imagination
how carefully and conscientiously a woman sculptor
must organize her hours in order to be an effective
person in so many lines. Member, so runs the illumi-
nating list, of the Framingham Woman's Club,
Framingham Civic League, Framingham Planning
Committee, American Federation of Arts, Federation of Women's Clubs (Art Committee), honor-
ary member, Alpha Kappa Alpha.

As her children have grown and her immediate
family cares have been less pressing, Mrs. Fuller,
like so many other women in similar circumstances,
has turned back to the absorbing interests of her
girlhood, now returning. Many another wife and
mother, reaching middle life, might echo her words
to me in a recent letter, "I was willing to give up

art and to be a good housewife, but is it possible for one who loves art and lives it, ever to renounce it for anything else?" Surely anyone who has not merely loved art but has come particularly to love the deep beauty and symbolism of the art of Meta Warrick Fuller, will be made glad and hopeful by these additional words from the same letter, "In 1929 I built a studio where I now work and enjoy to the full the time passed devoted to my work."

Here in this studio the sculptor sometimes returns to her early interest in the small figure, or sometimes makes, for example, a baptismal fount. One such is now placed in a church in Maine. She is also particularly successful in portraits—for the most part, plaques and bas-reliefs. Her portrait of Coleridge-Taylor has become widely known. She has created, also, a fine delineation of the face of Moorfield Storey, the great lawyer-friend of her people. But there is another aspect of Mrs. Fuller's present art activity less known but perhaps suggestive and appealing. From her little-girlhood on, Meta Warrick Fuller has always been a lover of home. Why should not every home, she asks, be made beautiful with objects of art, fresh and individual? So her fingers, still so clever with clay, do not always make objects for public exhibition; they like to fashion bits of beauty that may stand on the home table or shelf. A pair of recent book-ends reveals Mrs. Fuller's respect for domestic art, her desire to let beauty appear in handwork to be looked at not in an aloof art gallery, but in an everyday home. Simple as these book-ends are, they are perhaps significant. They hold together the tall, romance-packed volumes of

Percy's *Reliques*, all that magic of ballad poetry, as if they were somehow inclosing and offsetting with their peace all those intense young-girl fancies of a sculptor woman now grown older, quieter. A deep serenity of spirit pervades all Mrs. Fuller's work of today, revealing itself even in this pair of book-ends, articles so often cheap and grotesque. Looking at them, one stops to ponder this thought —if a woman has always chosen to be a person first, and an artist afterward, has she somehow thus gained a spirit of her own which she can't help putting into every smallest object produced by her gifted fingers? There stand those book-ends as an answer to this question. They show two faces, women's, in fine white profile against a dusky background. The faces look forth from graceful, cowl-like drapery. They are faces, small though they are, as soothing, as full of quiet and release, as some far-off evening light shining beyond brown tree trunks. "Book-ends" is a homely name for sculptured faces that can make you feel like that, but perhaps Mrs. Fuller meant to show that this is just the way all great and good books should make us feel, for she calls these two faces—the straight-gazing one, "Silence," and the other, a girl's face uplifted as if to evening stars, "Repose."

CHAPTER VI

CECILIA BEAUX,
PAINTER BEHIND THE PORTRAITS

OUT and in the rooms of our tiny school there used to flash some years ago a young girl so vivid that she seemed a flame. All was quiet until she entered. All was alive afterward. We teachers knew her for a mischief and a witch, but how we loved her! Her gleaming dark eyes, her eager slim figure, her definite gestures, were ours during school hours. Ernesta—I used to watch her and wish I might make a picture of her oval face or sketch her hands. I did not know that a great artist was already doing that, had been doing it since the little witch girl was a baby. I did not know that a few years later a great daily would carry in its rotogravure section a copy of a portrait of this young girl just grown to womanhood, a lovely flashing picture named quite simply "Ernesta."

All this was possible because the birth fairies had endowed Ernesta Drinker with an aunt so gifted and devoted that she was able to make a young girl alive upon canvas. And not only girl portraits have come from the brush of Cecilia Beaux, but portraits of famous and awe-inspiring world men.

The story of Cecilia Beaux and how and why she became an artist is an interesting one, and like

most good stories it begins before the heroine was
born. The lovely name Cecilia had been used by
her mother and by her grandmother before it came
to be hers; and in a way it was not hers because as a
child she was called Leilie. Her mother had lived
long enough after her birth to whisper the wish that
the baby daughter should bear the name Cecilia. It
was the child's grandmother, the first Cecilia, who
brought up little Leilie. The final name of Beaux
came, of course, from her French father. She received many things besides her name from the
French side of the family—the knowledge of a foreign tongue, the knowledge of beautiful French
hymns beloved of M. Beaux, the services in the
French church in Philadelphia where these hymns
were sung simply and solemnly. These entered
closely into the child's life and into the life of her
sister, Aimée Ernesta. The grandmother was helped
in her care of both little girls by two young aunts,
one of whom could sketch and paint. Cecilia Beaux
was a mite of a child when she took up a wood-
framed slate and drew on it a figure quickly recognized by the family as "the organ-grinder."

All life seemed to come to the child Leilie in pictures—the picture of the brisk, black-bonneted
grandmother on her way to market, the pictures of
other people she saw every day and of places she
only saw during the summer travels of the family.
The memory pictures of these summer sights were
of sails and sunrises and brooks and a quiet, friendly
farmhouse. The lovely country memories were only
of summer vacation months. The city housed the
family in winter until a move was made to West

Philadelphia, where at that time there were trees, outlying fields, and even a cool spring-house where the children might play. For rainy play days there was the little-used third story where quietness lived and where delightful books like *Gulliver's Travels* were to be found. Miss Beaux tells us in her recent biography that reading was best loved in the third-story stillness, but lessons took place in the dining-room at a table covered with green felt. In *Background with Figures* Cecilia Beaux looks back at her life and gives us glimpses of the girl she was and the girl she still is, for years cannot make really worth-while people lose their youthful outlook.

Idleness was unknown to the child Leilie. Belonging to a family interested in art and music, she was only a tiny thing when she could do part singing, but she did not find the piano easy to master. A family decision released her from long hours of practicing on the black-and-white keyboard of the old Chickering. Music came to Cecilia Beaux in her home; art came to her when she was taken to see exhibitions of famous pictures. Usually these art excursions were to the Pennsylvania Academy of Fine Arts in Philadelphia. The relatives who took the child to see the work of great artists let her wander about the corridors as she liked; they could not let her stay as long as she wished, for she would never have wished to leave. Leilie had no idea that she herself was ever to be an artist with pictures hanging on these very walls, but she knew she loved pictures and of course she had her favorite artists.

There were lessons as well as art and music in the little girl's life. Until she was fourteen these lessons were at home. Afterward she attended Miss Lyman's School in Philadelphia. Two years at a fashionable boarding-school did not change the ideals firmly set in Leilie's mind by her sensible grandmother. The ideals and the memories of her little-girlhood were beautiful and never forgotten. Looking back at them Cecilia Beaux writes, "Recollections of childhood have all the super-grace, the quality, the *patine* of the best antiques; their mystic beauty, their value as the furniture of the soul."

Always there was through these years of education an affluent and affectionate uncle watching the young girl's future. When special lessons were needed he stood ready to supply them. After Miss Lyman's there were art lessons. These were first given by Miss Katherine Drinker, a relative of Miss Beaux's uncle and a thoroughly talented and delightful person who later married Thomas A. Janvier, the writer. There was Miss Drinker's studio, of course, a delightful one on the top floor of an old Independence Square house. The studio was full of new life for the young artist. Many former artists had used its walls as sketching-ground. Partly faded crayon figures teased the imagination. Treasures from Chinese travel gave culture to the room; walls, curtains, and a skylight accentuated the shadows and the light—and light or the lack óf it has always been Cecilia Beaux's absorbing interest. There were people, too, in this enchanting studio— young Thomas Janvier and many other visitors. The young artist's work was to copy outline studies of Greek sculpture. Miss Drinker became deeply interested in her pupil and took her at times to her charming home and to the home of Mr. John Phillips, a collector of engravings.

When Miss Beaux was seventeen the devoted uncle found an art school fitted to her needs. A Dutch artist named Van der Whelen was giving instruction to a group of students in two large light rooms up many flights of Philadelphia stairs. The studio school was supplied with casts, easels, and a blackboard. Cecilia Beaux was set to copying lithographs, while her foreign instructor asked her if she had ever "enlairchet" anything. Her first task was to make a full-sized copy of a tiny picture of an old man. Crayon copies of plaster casts of Greek sculpture followed. After a little more than a year of this instruction Miss Beaux found the school changing hands. Her old teacher, Miss Drinker, now Mrs. Thomas A. Janvier, took charge. Mrs. Janvier recommended her former pupil to be art instructor at Miss Sanford's School, where she herself had taught.

Starting out as an inexperienced teacher, Cecilia Beaux was glad to find the school under good control and the work not difficult. Private pupils followed, but the devoted uncle does not seem to have been satisfied. He wished his niece to make progress in art. Since she had so frequently copied lithographs, he thought she might learn to make them herself, so he took her to a lithographing establishment where she first saw the stones on which the first drawings are made. Later she used these stones at home, making lithographs of fossils for the great scientist, Edward Drinker Cope. All this time the young copyist did not think of herself as an artist.

She read, however, with great liking, Ruskin's *Modern Painters*. Sometimes she did a crayon portrait of a friend or a relative. The interested uncle was opposed to the life class in most art schools, and it was some time before Miss Beaux had further instruction. Then through a friend she was invited to join an art class under the direction of William Sartain of New York. For two years this instruction continued and money enough came in through her brush and crayons for Cecilia Beaux to have her own studio at last. A portrait was hung at the Pennsylvania Academy and its reception was favorable.

About this time the vision of her earliest great picture came to Miss Beaux. But how was she to make it a reality? The figures in the portrait were to be Cecilia Beaux's sister and her little son. It was to be a picture of motherhood. But how to get her sister and the boy to sit for her was the artist's question. The sisters did not live in the same place. The young mother was limited in means and time. With the help of the family and friends, however, the sittings were accomplished and the lovely picture finished at last and named, *Les Derniers Jours d'Enfance*. Seated in a large low chair, the brooding young mother holds the dark-haired little lad carelessly and comfortably. The dark folds of the mother's dress are sharply contrasted with the boy's light play suit and rounded white knees. The mother's restful white hands lie under the boy's chubby fingers. The background for the seated figures is as restful as the faces of the mother and the little son. A bit of dark wainscoting, a darkly shining table, a richly figured rug and a jug with a blossom spray—these are all the great artist needed as setting for this lovely portrait of tranquil motherhood.

The finished picture went to the Pennsylvania Academy, then, strangely enough it accompanied a friend of Miss Beaux's to Paris, where, unheralded and by an unknown American artist, it captured a place in the Salon. After a lapse of months the portrait returned to its maker. Of its home-coming she writes, "The prodigal would never reveal the fiercely longed-for mysteries (of its trip). Perhaps it was better so, and it is probable that before the canvas, dumb as a granite door, was formed the purpose to go myself as soon as possible."

Savings and the ever-generous uncle brought about the desired European travel and instruction. A cousin companion was found and the voyage, a winter one, was accomplished. The life in Paris was studious, happy, and hard, but cold and quaintly inadequate lodgings did not chill the spirits of the young students. There were merry friendships and a wonderful world of paintings and people. To break the Paris life at times came trips to the country and farther, even to Lucerne and Venice and Florence, and most memorably to England in the spring of the second year in Paris. "I heard from an old friend in Cambridge," writes Miss Beaux, "an American girl who had married George, the eldest of the sons of Charles Darwin. She demanded a visit, and soon, as the gay season in Cambridge was approaching." There followed the delightful unfolding of a cultured English life such as Cecilia Beaux had met in books. From the first it was utterly charming to

her. A short stay in Paris was followed by a return
to Cambridge. In her studio, called "The Mill,"
Miss Beaux began to "do" portraits of famous English men and women.

The return to America brought renewed pleasure
in the life of the family and in the deepening of old
friendships. The family life was shadowed, however, by the failing strength of the exquisite and
indomitable grandmother. But there were still happy
hours when the loved one could walk about the
rooms assisted by her devoted Cecilia.

The date of the quiet passing of the exquisite old
grandmother marked reconstruction days in America. A group of far-seeing people wished to secure
historical art treasures for their country. Five artists were chosen to go to Europe and paint portraits
of the great of the Great War. Three people were
allotted to each artist. Cecilia Beaux was one of the
five artists and the three great men who fell to her
share were Cardinal Mercier, Clemenceau, and the
English hero, Lord Beatty.

No great man ever had a more interested portrait-
painter than Cecilia Beaux. She deeply appreciated
her opportunities for knowing these three men of
the World War. In her autobiography she writes
first of the greatly loved and greatly loving Cardinal, "I always felt," she says, "that the Tower (of
Malines) was the architectural type of the Cardinal,
a supreme example of simplicity in richness, height
and depth, full of holy joy, like the carolling of the
upper bells, and with the profound resonance and
majesty of the greatest bell of all, and the most
moving, which I one day heard tolling with its deep

voice the years of a life." And the woman who painted this wonderful word picture of Cardinal Mercier placed him just as wonderfully on canvas and even more indelibly. In the portrait the Cardinal's tall figure is slightly bent forward. The robes of his office are dignified but not ornate. The face shows an exquisite openness reinforced with intellectuality.

From the Cardinal to Clemenceau, that is how the portraits follow one another in Miss Beaux's book. The two men were immensely different, but as the artist says, "All except a few irremediably perverse minds cease to argue when humanity reaches beyond the normal heights. In the few authoritative indications inscribed high up upon the cliffs of History, these two diverse thinkers appear under the same signs; signs beyond our vision, only heard of by us, for they do not indicate the germs and shoots of qualities it is to be hoped we all possess, but the supreme development of those qualities. How well we know their titles!—Patriotism, Faith, Courage, and Endurance."

Clemenceau's was a face long familiar to the public, but it was not a face easily accessible to the artist. A great statesman at the close of a great war had many things to do besides sitting for his portrait. But at last the treaty was signed and Miss Beaux was given a ticket entitling her to be present when Clemenceau read the document to the governing body of France. She writes, "The impression of Clemenceau in the Tribune, facing a partly hostile audience (hostile, at least, to the treaty, for all France now knew and either feared or adored his strength), took all one's capacity for absorption. More could not be carried away."

Months intervened before the artist secured sittings of the great statesman in his own home. Their opening conversation was memorable.

" 'Well, to begin with, we hate one another,' " said the great man.

The artist's answer was received with a laugh. "No, monsieur, that is only half true." It later became wholly untrue as the work progressed most successfully.

Clemenceau had called Lord Beatty "a British sailor." Miss Beaux found the English Admiral considerate. Of him she says: "Lord Beatty was prompt for his appointment, as might have been expected, and I asked for only time enough to make a few decisions in regard to position and lighting.— I saw that it was a falcon face; the nose broad at the base, unbelievably fine at the end, the brows bending toward it, eyelids heavy and full over large, far-seeing gray eyes. A falcon ready for the chase."

In the portrait Lord Beatty stands quietly fronting the world, his uniform upon him and his hands resting upon his sword.

Years before Cecilia Beaux went to Europe to make her famous war portraits she had made herself a home near Gloucester, Massachusetts. Because of the trees and other greenery about the place she named it "Green Alley." "On the evening of August 7, 1906, the first fire was kindled on the hearth at Green Alley," she writes, "and I made a feint of sleeping there that night." She has slept there many nights since. And she has worked there.

"Work," she writes; "I never exhausted the resources of the studio. Many half-conceived designs are waiting under its dark rafters, and in the moteful shafts of light from its high east window."

And still Cecilia Beaux goes on working, growing ever more understanding and efficient. The people in her portraits will never be forgotten so long as the canvases live; and she herself will always be remembered for her great gift of making true pictures of true people.

CHAPTER VII

MADAME LE BRUN,
PLAYMATE OF MARIE ANTOINETTE

"I DO not know much about painting, but you make me love it," King Louis XVI said to the talented Madame Le Brun. And the girl who made a king love painting has made many others love her art—because she loved it herself.

Picture Marie Louise Elizabeth Vigée away back in 1760, a little maid of five, in an old Parisian convent school, decorating the stately walls with her colored chalks; she made trouble, of course, with her unappreciated murals, but she was quite merry about it and she didn't stop drawing. The word *stop* was never in her language. At home she even attempted a portrait study, the head of a man. In her life story called *Souvenirs* Madame Le Brun tells us she was glad to leave the convent when she was eleven years old—probably she would have been glad to leave it sooner had circumstances been willing.

It has been said by a famous Frenchman that, "All the fairies gathered about the cradle of Elizabeth Vigée, as for the birth of a little princess in the kingdom of art. One gave her beauty, another genius; the fairy Gracious offered her a pencil and a palette. The fairy of marriage, who had not been

69

summoned, told her, it is true, that she should wed
M. Le Brun, the expert in pictures—but for her
consolation the fairy of travelers promised her that
she should bear from court to court, from academy
to academy, from Paris to Petersburg, and from
Rome to London, her gaiety, her talent, and her
easel—before which all the sovereigns of Europe
and all those whom genius had crowned should place
themselves as subjects for her brush."

And the little girl at whose birth fairies were so
generous stopped going to school when she was
eleven years old! Her education was considered
complete except in art. She was first taught painting
by her artist father, and later benefited by the advice of Doyen, Greuze, and Vernet. When little
Elizabeth was thirteen years old her devoted father
died. For some time the young artist was so grief-
stricken that she could not paint at all. To cheer
her and get her mind back on her work, she was
taken to see the paintings of Rubens and other
great artists. The slender little girl with the wide-
set, wondering eyes found in the art-galleries what
her father had found, comfort and inspiration and
happiness, in a world of beauty.

At fifteen Elizabeth Vigée was quite definitely
beautiful, though she tells us modestly that her
younger brother was "prettier than she." The little
artist was much more than good to look upon; she
was a successful and very busy portrait painter.
Older and less successful artists watched the stream
of well-known people crowding her studio doors.
They could not understand how a mere girl could
win people and fame. But she did it. And she was

no young, early-flowering prodigy merely; she kept right on winning friends and fame through a long, long lifetime of art.

There were changes in the home circle; an unfortunate and disagreeable stepfather replaced the dearly loved M. Vigée. But now that Elizabeth had gone back to work she wasn't going to let home conditions worry her. She set herself to help support the family—and she did it.

In 1776 she married the art critic, M. Le Brun, a man older than herself and much more interested in money than in his talented girl-wife. Marriage did not mean that Madame Le Brun gave up her work. She merely worked harder because she had a husband to spend her earnings. Fortunately, she always loved painting and she always loved her friends. In 1780 she had a charming little daughter to love. Life seemed very full and happy. Fame increased, and in 1783 the painting "Peace Bringing Back Abundance" gained Vigée Le Brun membership in the French Academy. She was young, she was lovely, she was famous, and she had many friends. Poets made verses about the clever artist. She was the center of a brilliant group, but somehow she managed to keep hard at work; art was always first with her. She often sat at her easel all day long, receiving her callers in her studio, but not leaving her painting until evening, when she often gave supper parties. At these entertainments conversation kept pace with novel forms of enjoyment. There was the famous Greek supper, so severely censured by the critics. In fact, critics seem to have been even busier then than they are today. Anyone who had as many friends as Madame Le Brun could not escape having also envious enemies. Her critics said the Greek supper had been extravagant. They even ran to the king and complained of the bad example Vigée Le Brun was setting France. But the gay little artist had not been a spendthrift; she had merely been very clever. There were no elaborate preparations for the famous meal. It was a spur-of-the-moment affair. Word was hastily sent to friends to appear in Greek costume. The Greek ornaments in the studio were brought forward and the cook was told how to serve simple Greek viands. Some one read Greek poetry. The hostess spent—well, the sum has been set at fifteen francs. But what a fuss Paris made over that successful supper! The hard-working artist was dubbed extravagant for all time; but she does not seem to have become bitter under this harsh judgment, or under the envy and unkindness of those less gifted than herself. Madame Le Brun's disposition seems to have been puncture-proof. She was free because she really didn't care what people said about her, but perhaps she was not easily hurt herself, because she never seems to have wished to hurt other people. She did not have to waste any time in regretting slights she paid other people; she did not slight anyone, because hers was not the little world of "getting even" but the big world of getting on in art.

And then there were always many, many friends for Madame Le Brun to think about. She really couldn't waste her mind on her enemies when she had a queen for her playmate. Marie Antoinette and Vigée Le Brun were about the same age and they were both fond of music and very fond of children. It was a red-letter day in the palace when they sang duets together. When the royal portraits were being painted the queen and the artist made their friendship firm and lasting. Madame Le Brun painted many portraits of the queen. With all her warm heart and radiant nature she grew to love the royal family of France, as she painted them one by one, sometimes alone, sometimes in groups. Did she ever feel, as she held her busy brush, that this affection was to be pierced with pain? When she reproduced the wistful face of the little dauphin did she have any premonition of what life was to hold for him?

Perhaps she had, for if she had not been quick-witted and resourceful, fate might have held for her the same tragic death. When the rumblings of the French Revolution became insistent in 1789 Vigée Le Brun escaped with her little daughter and a faithful servant. Of course she did not make her escape as Madame Le Brun, the artist; she was far too well-known at the court for that to have been done safely. Many officials in France were familiar with her self-portraits and almost everyone today knows one or more of these pictures—the graceful head above the slender neck, the eager eyes and lovely features, the quaint head-dresses with the piquant touch, the lovely hands, sometimes holding a brush or palette, but more often clasping the artist's lovely little daughter. This woman was entirely too famous to make her escape from France without a disguise—and she made one in a hurry. No one knew her in her workingwoman's dress. No one knew she had left a canvas and a paint-brush wet in her studio and set out on a long series of famous adventures. She looked merely like any servant traveling in a public carriage between a thief and a Jacobin. All reached the border safely.

The artist set out toward the south, and for her it proved a land of promise. Her art was known and she found cities ready to welcome her and give her what she wanted, portrait-work. At Turin she was a distinguished guest; at Bologna she speedily became a member of the Academy, and the city of Florence, besides asking her to paint portraits of other famous people, insisted that she leave a portrait of herself in the Uffizi. Not far away, as wall space goes, in the same great gallery hangs the self-portrait of another girl artist of an earlier day, the famous Angelica Kauffmann. What thoughts were in the minds of the two girl artists as they painted these portraits to be hung in the Uffizi? Perhaps they were thinking of the girls of the future who might stand before the pictures and wonder what it would be like to reach a dream—to be so famous that a great city would wish a self-portrait for its very own. Perhaps the two painters were not thinking of the future at all and of the message of hope and of dreams come true through hard work. But whatever was in their minds, the message is there for people of today, the good news of the conquest of poverty and hard circumstances.

The art-filled city of Florence did not outdo Rome in paying tribute to Madame Le Brun. She was entertained and applauded and given what she most wanted in the old Roman capital—her own kind of work. Her paint-brush was always busy. In fact it had never been idle since at fifteen she had begun to earn a fair-sized income at her easel. The harder she worked the happier she was. To her, painting was not a big burden tied on her slender shoulders as she traveled from city to city. Just because she had to paint she did not hate it. And Vigée Le Brun had to work, there wasn't the least doubt in the world about that. She had brought a very small amount of money from France because her escape had been a hasty one. She cheerfully set about earning more.

Naples followed Rome in Madame Le Brun's travels. In Naples she painted Lady Hamilton as a Bacchante and as a Sybil. In Naples, also, she painted Paisiello, a portrait which later gained the praise of the painter David. The Queen of Naples and her relatives were charmed with the gay French artist, for wherever there was a queen Madame Le Brun seems to have found her out and made friends with her and painted her portrait. The story of the beautiful refugee reads like a fairy tale. Instead of pitying herself because she was an exile from her home and from her dearly beloved France, Madame Le Brun went right to work and set up her easel and made friends and was happy—and as everyone knows a busy happy person is bound to be popular whether she is a long-ago artist or a girl of today.

After three years in Italy there came news from the homeland that saddened the valiant and loyal heart of Vigée Le Brun. Her dear friend and queen, Marie Antoinette, and all the royal French family had been put to death by the guillotine. Many of

the artist's friends had met a like fate. The blow
was terrible; there was nothing but work to ease the
pain. Madame Le Brun packed her easel once more
and set it up again in Vienna. There she was warmly
welcomed and the same sort of life went on to which
she had already become accustomed in Italy—great
people sought her out, she was praised, she had work
to do, she was able to earn a good income.

But no city could hold the French artist very long.
In her homesick heart she must have been thinking
of the Paris that had been hers. She grew restless
and left Vienna for Prague, and from there she
went to Dresden and Berlin. In July, 1795, Madame
Le Brun went to St. Petersburg. There she found a
number of French refugees, and there she felt at
home. Of course she went right to work painting
portraits of famous people and making friends as
she had always done. For six years this life went
on. There were portraits of the royal children and
there was to have been a picture of the Empress
Catherine, but the old lady was suddenly taken
fatally ill. There were portraits and portraits to be
painted, however, and thrifty Madame Le Brun
saved the sums they brought her. She became rich,
but she didn't stop working. Although an exile, she
was a great lady in Russia, and all St. Petersburg
turned out to do her honor when she was made a
member of the Russian Academy.

The hard-won Russian happiness was soon torn
in pieces by an unexpected misfortune. The lovely
little daughter of the French artist had traveled with
her famous mother from city to city and her mother
was scarcely aware that she had grown up when

she engaged herself to a Russian diplomat quite unworthy of her love. Madame Le Brun tried to prevent the match, but she couldn't. In her sorrow she turned back to her beloved Paris, but it wasn't in the least like the Paris she had left. She had come by way of Moscow and Berlin, where Queen Louise was most kind and where Vigée Le Brun must have been reminded of her dear queen-friend, Marie Antoinette. But there weren't any queens in France. Napoleon had been First Consul for a year when the artist reached her native city. She was lonely, though her husband gave her a hearty welcome. In her distress she sought new friends in London. Of course she found them. Lord Byron and others crowded to sit for the French painter. Sir Joshua Reynolds, the great English portrait-painter, became interested in the traveled exile. Madame Le Brun tried to be happy, but she was estranged from her dearly loved daughter and the noise of London drove her frantic. She moved from lodging to lodging but couldn't find a comfortable place to paint. In 1805 she returned to Paris by way of Holland. She hoped to see her daughter, now married to her chosen Russian. The meeting was not a happy one. The loving, self-sacrificing mother found that the girl for whom she had done so much did not really love her. People might fail Madame Le Brun, but painting never did. Painting was good medicine for any trouble. She set out on a journey to Switzerland to paint, not people, but places. But portraits were always to be Madame Le Brun's best-known work. She returned after a time to Paris and bought a country house at Louveciennes, near enough to the city for her friends to come to her. Afterwards until her death in 1842 she divided her time between Paris and the country. Her travels were over, but not her work.

In 1813 Madame Le Brun's husband died and in 1819 her daughter passed away. Affectionate and forgiving, Vigée Le Brun mourned sincerely for both her loved ones. Two nieces cared for her during her own declining years. She died in Paris when she was eighty-seven years old. Her lovely paintings still live. It has been said of Madame Le Brun that she was the first woman in France, since the time of Queen Matilda of the Bayeux tapestries, to be publicly recognized as a painter. She will always be recognized wherever her story is known as a brave woman and an indomitable worker.

CHAPTER VIII

ANGELICA KAUFFMANN, THE PICTURE-WORKER

WHEN Angelica Kauffmann was born in 1742 it almost seemed as if her artist father's paint-brush had slipped right into her baby fingers, so early did she begin to paint. Mr. Kauffmann had gone to Coire, Switzerland, to paint frescoes in a church. There he had met and married Angelica's lovely mother; but Coire was not to be a permanent home. When the prodigy baby was one year old the Kauffmann family made the first of their many moves. The new home town was Morbegno in Lombardy. There little Angelica painted and also showed a decided talent for music. When she was eleven years old the second home was left behind and a new one was made in Como, where the talented child had expert instruction in both music and painting. Later in life when Angelica painted portraits of herself, one of them showed her as a bewildered child set between two mythical figures, one Music, the other Painting. She always remembered how hard it had been for her to make her life choice. Her music did not go entirely into the discard, however, for she always delighted her many friends by her lovely singing voice.

Milan followed Como in the list of Kauffmann

homes, and to every artist, young and old, Milan
means the master painter, Leonardo da Vinci. Angelica studied the artist's wonderful work, com-
pleted so many years before her own was begun.
She marveled at the rich coloring, the depth of
expression in the beautiful faces, the grouping of
the figures, the artist's wonderful plan in each
painting and fresco. Not only Leonardo's paintings,
but those of other artists, made the young student
work even more eagerly in Milan than she had in
Como.

Angelica's pictures soon showed the depth of her
eagerness and energy. They won the notice of Robert d'Este, who interested the Duchess Carrara in
his young protégée. The busy and brilliant life into
which the little artist now entered was in abrupt
contrast to what followed closely. Angelica's mother
died and her sorrowing father decided to return to
his birthplace, Schwarzenburg, and occupy himself
in doing decorative work there. Life in Schwarzenburg was plain and rough and unlovely in many ways.
There were new hardships and there was piercing
grief for the lovely dead mother, but there was
beauty, too, of a sort quite different from Milan—
beauty of the strong, wind-swept pine trees of the
north country, and there was work. It was a very
special sort of work and most unusual for a young
girl of Angelica Kauffmann's age, or even of ours.
She decorated the interior of a church with figures
of the twelve apostles as the artist Piazetta had
earlier interpreted them.

The stay in Schwarzenburg came to an end
quickly, and again Angelica found herself making a

new home for her restless father. It was Milan once more, then an interval of study in Florence; and when the girl artist had become an accomplished painter, although only eighteen years old, fate and her father took her to Rome. She was used to small city life, she was used to country life, she was used to people, but best of all she was quite used to work. Always during the family wanderings she had chosen the best in each new environment and she had always set to work promptly as soon as she had established herself in a new home. Angelica Kauffmann was ready for Rome, and Rome was ready for the beautiful talented girl with the lovely singing voice. She was utterly friendly, and people of note were quickly interested in her. A very great man became constructively kind to her. Winckelmann, the great German archæologist and historian of classic art, was now in Rome. He had been the son of a poor shoemaker and had risen in life by his own efforts. He was ready, now, as an elderly and famous man, to lend a hand to others who were trying to perfect themselves in some branch of art or learning. To Angelica Kauffmann, Winckelmann was especially kind and understanding. He allowed her to paint his portrait and, having such a famous man sit for her, gave the young artist many more opportunities for making portraits in the Italian capital. Foreigners came to her because she had not confined her studies to art. She had made the most of her good opportunities for learning different languages. She could speak French, German, Italian, and English. Her knowledge of English brought her the friendship of Lady Wentworth, with whom she afterward went to England. But before her interesting London life there came visits to Naples, Bologna, Venice, and Paris. When the girl artist reached London she was described as "not very tall, but slight, and her figure well-proportioned. She had a dark, clear complexion, a gracious mouth, white and equal teeth, and well-marked features; above all, her azure eyes, so placid and so bright, charmed you with an expression it is impossible to write; unless you had known her you could not understand how eloquent were her looks."

One of her self-portraits shows Angelica Kauffmann seated, pencil in hand, evidently looking at some one else she is about to sketch. The face and throat and hands are very beautiful, but there is something entirely self-forgetful in the pose. The picture is Angelica at work, absorbed in her art, utterly unaware of her own loveliness, quite willing that people should forget all about her if they would remember her pictures.

Nowadays a career is something many a girl wishes and achieves, but in the eighteenth century few girls were sufficiently independent and industrious to attain skill and fame in art or in anything else. Angelica seems to have kept all her womanly charm while doing work usually considered the work of a man. So London found the young artist busy, devoted to her art, but not unwilling to give time and affection to her friends. The royal family added themselves to the group of famous people surrounding the newly-arrived painter. The king's mother did her the honor of visiting her. The Princess of Brunswick wished several pictures painted. Other people of rank also gave her orders. She felt prosperous and began to think of the time when she might be able to provide a permanent home for her restless father. She seemed to be gaining fame and fortune, with few obstacles in her busy path. She was chosen without question as one of the original members of the Royal Academy. Sir Joshua Reynolds was her friend and even called her "Miss Angel." He painted her portrait and she in turn painted his, and also a portrait of the most famous actor of that time, David Garrick.

The future of the young artist seemed altogether bright and beautiful and then it was marred by a mistake—her own. The girl who had made no error in choosing her career made a sad mistake in choosing a husband. She had many offers, but she married in secret a man who pretended to be what he was not, the Count de Horn. Angelica confided the secret of her marriage to Queen Charlotte, whose portrait she was painting. The friendly Queen wished to have the count presented at court. When inquiries were made it was found that Angelica had been deceived; instead of a count she had married a wicked adventurer. She left him when it was found that he had a living wife. At this sad time of her life Angelica's work was her greatest comfort, as it had also been during her prosperity. Seeing her keeping bravely at work, her friends were even more devoted than before. For twelve years Angelica Kauffmann worked hard and supported herself and her father in London. In 1781 her father's ill health made a return to Italy advisable. In Italy she married an old and very faithful friend, Antonio Zucchi, also an artist.

Her husband had a home in Rome and Angelica made it a center of literary and artistic life. Like herself, Antonio Zucchi was a member of the Royal Academy in London. This has been said of them: "It was interesting to see Angelica and her husband before a picture. While Zucchi spoke with enthusiasm, Angelica remained silent, fixing her eloquent gaze on the finest portions of the work. In her countenance one could read her emotions, while her observations were limited to a few brief words. These, however, seldom expressed any blame—only the praises of that which was worthy of praise. It belonged to her nature to recognize the beauty alone —as the bee draws honey only out of every flower."

As to her own work, Goethe has written of her, "The good Angelica has a most remarkable, and for a woman unheard-of, talent; one must see and value what she does and not what she leaves undone. There is much to learn from her, particularly as to work, for what she affects is really marvelous."

Not even a wealthy and devoted husband could make Angelica Kauffmann neglect her chosen art. Antonio Zucchi bought a charming villa at Castle Gondolfo, hoping to persuade his wife to be more often idle, but she was never quite happy when she was long away from her studio in Rome. In 1795 this happy married life came to an end with the death of Signor Zucchi. Angelica survived him by twelve increasingly sad years. She tried to find happiness in revisiting the scenes of her youthful travels, but only her work in Rome brought her peace.

She died at last in Rome, and her impressive funeral showed in what great esteem she was held. Angelica Kauffmann was buried in Sant' Andrea dei Frati at her husband's side. Her latest paintings were carried in the funeral procession and all Rome mourned her sincerely. Her bust was placed in the Pantheon.

The many famous pictures painted by this industrious and gifted artist are scattered over Europe in various picture-galleries. On the margin of one of her pictures she wrote, "I will not attempt to express supernatural things by human inspiration, but wait for that till I reach heaven, if there is painting done there."

A few of Angelica Kauffmann's pictures, however, are of religious subjects. "Madonna in Glory" and "Woman of Samaria" are in Munich. A "Holy Family" is in Venice. Many of the paintings are of classical theme—Virgil, Achilles, Pallas—all were painted by Angelica. She also, of course, painted many contemporary portraits, as, "Portrait of a Lady in Stuttgart" and that of the Duchess of Brunswick at Hampton Court Palace. There are also self-portraits in Berlin, Munich, Innsbruck, and Philadelphia, London and Florence. In Dresden are "Ariadne," "A Young Sybil and a Young Vestal."

Among women painters Angelica Kauffmann will always have a place because of her talent, her achievements, her friendships, and her true womanhood.

CHAPTER IX

JANET SCUDDER,
A GIRL WHO MADE HER OWN NAME

WE OFTEN hear of self-made men. The written lives of most great men begin with the statement that as a boy the noted man rose above his surroundings. But who has heard of a self-made girl? There are some, however, and this is the story of a very spirited girl, Janet Scudder, who has become a famous sculptor. In the first place Janet Scudder made herself a name because she did not like the name her mother's friend had given her. And neither would you have liked to be Netta Deweze Frazee. In childhood it wasn't so bad to be Netta, Net, or Nettie; but when she was eighteen and a student in the Cincinnati Academy of Art Miss Scudder just had to have a new first name. She was told, on entering the Academy, that Netta wasn't a name at all, so she tried Antoinette and Jeanette and at last Janet. She has been Janet ever since.

But before she was Janet she had to be Netta for eighteen years, beginning somewhere in the 1870's as to years, and as to place—well, Terre Haute, Indiana, is the lucky town that was Janet Scudder's birthplace and girlhood home. It wasn't a happy home for little Netta because Poverty was spelled in it with a very large *P*. And there weren't

86

any letters to spell M-O-T-H-E-R because Netta's mother was dead. Later, when Netta was going to school there was a rather tragic stepmother. Of course, Netta's home held, besides its sadness, some elements of cheer; she loved the quiet father who pinned her first picture on the wall where he might see it when he took his daily nap; Hannah Hussey, too, was a joy, big and broad and Irish and capable of doing much more than the Scudder cooking; she did the comforting as well. Hannah had confidence in little Netta's talents; so had Caroline, Netta's school friend. Caroline suggested prize-winning exhibits at the county fair. Together the two girls carried off all the available prizes in art. Their pleasure was not marred when they found no other artists had competed.

But just because she could paint, Netta Scudder wasn't one-sided. She didn't sit with a paint-brush in her hand all day; she was thoroughly athletic, so much so that her brother said to her: "You are making a regular tomboy of yourself. The other boys don't like you that way. They say you want to run all their games, and they don't want you to. If you'll take my advice, you'll cut out all this silly gymnastic stuff at once."

The "gymnastic stuff," however, had made Netta strong and she found she needed all her mental and physical muscles when she carried through her first year's study at the Cincinnati Academy of Art. She studied muscles; even the muscles of a corpse came in person into the anatomy course Janet was taking. And the names of the muscles were many and long. Only one name stuck in the future sculptor's memory—gastrocnemius; to her it seemed the tennis muscle, and she's had experience with it. Muscles—there seemed to be nothing in Janet Scudder's world but muscles; then one day when she was quite tired of anatomy she chanced upon something she liked. Suppose we let her tell the story in her own words right from her book *Modeling My Life*: "Gradually it came over me that I was standing in the sculpture class-room, and with this knowledge came a flaring resentment that no one had ever told me it existed. There I had been studying all those other things for months and not even hearing about this branch of art."

Miss Scudder's first piece of sculpture was near to life and to earth—it was a model of a human foot. She had been pinching and patting that clay foot into shape for three weeks when a fellow student suggested casting it. A long piece of strong thread was laid down the center of the foot. Then plaster was mixed and colored blue with a small ball of coloring matter. The clay foot was covered first with blue plaster; before this hardened the thread was carefully pulled up, leaving a small open seam, then a white mixture was put over the blue, but the seam was never covered. When the second coat hardened a chisel was gently used in the seam cavity and the two halves of the mold of the foot fell apart. The mold was washed and oiled and tied tightly, leaving an opening at the top into which plaster was poured. The next day the mold was carefully chipped away, leaving Janet Scudder's first piece of sculpture. She never forgot her joy in this achievement.

Miss Scudder has modeled many feet since that first one—children's lovely bare feet and bodies and faces—for her most noted work has been the making of beautiful laughing child fountains that seem to dance and sing for joy.

While she was studying in Cincinnati the girl sculptor helped to support herself by wood-carving. Bread-trenchers and bookracks were fashionable, and consequently marketable. There was even an ornate mantelpiece that actually brought its maker sixty dollars for its carved grapes and curlicues.

Wood-carving, however, meant little to Miss Scudder after she had discovered clay. She hoped she had talent enough to become a really worthwhile sculptor, so she asked her teacher to be quite frank with her. He was. This is what he said: "I'm going to tell you something. You've got it in you— the feeling for clay—the understanding—the—well, whatever you want to call it! One of these days you will be a much greater sculptor than I am. You are going way beyond me."

And she has gone way beyond many sculptors, that girl who has made her own name. But it wasn't easy. Going beyond in anything is never easy. Her "understanding" helped her, and it isn't only the understanding of clay, it's the understanding of people, too, and of circumstances. The girl art student had plenty of hard circumstances and hard people to meet. Her father's death cut deeply into her affections and plans, but an older brother helped her to go on with her studies in Cincinnati and later invited her to live in his home in Chicago and find work in her "chosen profession."

It was wood-carving, however, not sculpture, that Janet Scudder first found in Chicago, factory work, but at a good salary. Labor troubles forced her to resign her position. What next? At first there didn't seem to be any next thing; but there had to be work, because brother was poor and Janet herself ambitious and of an independent spirit. "Help Wanted" columns did not seem to want her. At last she heard that the famous sculptor, Lorado Taft, was looking for assistants in his studio. Again there was a job in Janet's pocket. Again she began to make a name for herself by her old methods— eagerness, energy, willingness to do hard work, even to carrying pails of water for other sculptors. A name is never made easily. Janet Scudder describes in detail what the work of a studio assistant was. She writes, "The design for a group or statue is first made in a small sketch; from this sketch the sculptor models a very careful study in clay, usually one-fourth the size the finished work is to be; this is cast; over the plaster model is built a wooden frame, and from the top crosspieces strings are attached which fall to the floor. Beside this caged-in model is built another frame containing the iron armature—the framework on which the enlarged statue is to be built up. Then by means of a compass the distance from the strings to the clay model is measured, multiplied by four, and sticks reproducing this measurement are attached to the armature and extend to the point which is to be covered with clay." This building up, or "pointing" up, of statues was the work of the assistants. It was congenial work and there was plenty of it. There were delightful friendships to be made among the other workers. Janet Scudder especially enjoyed Mr. Taft's gifted sister Zulh.

It was a busy life at all times, but when the World's Fair entered it a wonderful year began for the studio assistants. The whole force moved to the Horticultural Building on the Fair grounds. A small hotel near by housed and fed the busy art workers, among whom were Bessie Potter Vonnoh, Enid Yandell, Caroline Brooks, and Zulh Taft. The hours were long, but filled with eager effort. When the first pay-envelopes were opened Janet Scudder and her friends hurried to their hotel room and spread out their five-dollar bills—the pay came that way—spread them right on the floor so that they might "see how it felt to walk on money."

The young sculptors found their work and one another absorbingly interesting, and the exposition world growing up around them was fascinating, too. Surely Janet Scudder had a thrill resembling that of Columbus when one day she watched a group of men erecting a plaster boat. Figures of women were at the oars, a Victory stood in the center. There was a lift of joy and nobility about the whole. Janet was wild to know the name of the originator of the glorious group. She made inquiries of the workmen and found the sculptor was "a gent in Paris," Mac-Monnies by name. She even found that the great man was present, watching the Chicago launching of his boat. Janet Scudder looked at him from afar, but did not dare to make his acquaintance. She did, however, register a resolution to become his pupil.

Two statues came between this pledge and its

immediate fulfillment. Lorado Taft had the state-building statues on his hands and it fell to Miss Scudder's lot to do "Justice" for the Illinois building. She was happily employed making the clay beginnings of this statue when a hometown letter from Terre Haute reached her. The letter offered her $1,000 if she would make a statue for the Indiana building. She accepted and completed both statues, but she writes of them: "Those two statues! I tremble now when I think what they must have been like. The Indiana one, called 'Nymph of the Wabash,' was packed up after the Fair closed and sent to Terre Haute and placed in the Public Library, where I am told it still stands, now principally coats of paint which have been given it each year to renew its youth. I have never had the courage to go and see it. Nothing in the world would make me. And I only regret it didn't have the same fate as 'Justice,' which was destroyed by fire."

After the work was all done and the Fair opened, Janet Scudder stayed on at the little hotel long enough to enjoy the Exposition. The girl who had never traveled felt as if the whole world had come to her. But beautiful as the World's Fair was it did not check her decision to go to Paris, and for Janet Scudder Paris meant MacMonnies and lessons in art. Of course she reached her wish. Zulh Taft went with her.

"Paris!" writes Miss Scudder, "I knew that first night that I loved it; and I have gone on loving it ever since."

It had been hard to reach Paris. It was harder to reach Frederick MacMonnies and to secure his consent to take a pupil. He frankly did not give lessons, but at last he consented to take Miss Scudder as a studio assistant to whom he gave advice. Eventually she helped the great sculptor in making the coat for the statue of Shakespeare now in the Congressional Library in Washington. It took three months of hard work to make that richly embroidered coat. Miss Scudder liked better her work on horses of the Quadriga, the beautiful sculptured group that tops the great arch at the entrance of Prospect Park in Brooklyn.

When Janet Scudder returned to America and tried to find work in New York, she discovered that even her letters of introduction to Saint-Gaudens could not secure employment for her at once. She spent a brave summer eating beans and drinking milk and holding on to her resolution to make her name mean something. The name Janet Scudder now means something in fortitude as well as in art. What girl who was not dogged could have stood this régime:

"Studio rent by month.........$14.00
Square meal every other day, for
    month ....$ 4.00
Milk, beans, bread...........$ 9.00

"There were literally no other expenses. I did my own washing. I never took a street car unless I was actually worn out. And it goes without saying that I never bought anything, least of all clothes."

Existing in this meager way Janet Scudder managed to wring a living out of New York, but as soon as she could scrape together enough money

she went back to Paris. Her friend, Matilda
Brownell, went with her, and with Matilda went
Parot, a very efficient French housekeeper-maid.
The three had a tiny Paris house with a ground-
floor studio. There Janet Scudder worked for three
years and there during those happy studious months
she says she "found herself." There was the Louvre,
there was music and there were boat trips on the
Seine. And all the time the young sculptor was working and asking herself just what branch of sculpture
was to be hers for life. Should it be grave or gay,
historical or fanciful? Janet Scudder didn't exactly
like to make monuments for cemeteries, but sometimes she made them. She enjoyed making a lively
figure called "Music" for the Paris Exposition, and
she was greatly encouraged when MacMonnies
showed some medallions of hers to the curator of
the Luxembourg Museum. "Would you mind giving
them to the French Government?" the young sculptor was asked. Never was a gift more cheerfully
given.

During the three "finding" years there were trips
to London, to different parts of France and most
memorably to Italy, where in the Bargello in Florence she became acquainted with the grace and joy
and beauty of Donatello's work. There in a mo-
ment she knew what she wanted to do. She wished
to make lovely, graceful, gay children come alive in
little statues. A visit to Naples and Pompeii made
her realize the loveliness of the fountain statuette.
She writes of this experience in deciding her life
work: "My work should please and amuse the world.

. . . My work was going to decorate spots, make
people feel cheerful and gay—nothing more!"

But into her gay determination broke the rumblings of the World War! Fortunately, Janet Scudder, through the help of Parot, had found a charming little boy model and made her famous Frog
Fountain. And when she returned to New York she
sold that fountain to the famous architect, Stanford
White, sold it right in the middle of the traffic of
Forty-second Street—sold it for one thousand dollars! Soon the lovely boy of the Frog Fountain had
little brother and sister fountains as fine as himself
in charming gardens belonging to the estates of famous Americans.

And still there was that horrible World War
coming closer and closer to America and ready to
take all the gaiety and joy out of statue-making.
Miss Scudder is far too sympathetic a woman not
to have laid aside her own work, charming as it was,
to aid the soldiers. She lectured for them and it was
about the hardest thing she could have done, for
from her school days public speaking of any kind
had seemed quite horrible to her. But she did it,
and did it well we may be sure. It helped her to feel
she was doing her part in the relief work.

But no matter how many speeches she made, Janet
Scudder could not forget those lovely children in
her brain waiting to be made into lasting statuary.
Somehow they were made, some of them in this
country and some of them in Paris. They have lovely
names, these fountain children—only a girl who has
named herself could have thought of the names—

"Young Diana," "Boy with Fish," "Little Lady from the Sea," "Young Pan," "Victory Statuette."

Young Diana is standing on one sandaled foot, her bow is in her hand and her lovely little face is turned intently toward the arrow she has just sent on its flight. Oh yes, everyone is sure the arrow is winging its way somewhere, for Young Diana is so lifelike one almost hears the twang of her bow-string. The "Boy with Fish" is real, too, he's a chubby little boy and the fish in his arms is a big one, but he will never let it go. "Little Lady from the Sea" is stepping backward up the rocks. Her eyes are still on the water and above her bent head she raises dripping seaweed. "Young Pan" is making music. His chubby feet are almost keeping time to it. His lovely tune rings in the mind.

These are only a few of Miss Scudder's dream children. With her eyes on a little faun she has made she writes of fountain children: "You, my little faun child, and all your brothers and sisters and cousins created before you, may not always be important; in your turn you may be cast into the scrapheap; but at least you have helped to open up a vast field in American sculpture—in creating you I have blazed a trail along which many American sculptors are now happily traveling. Garden sculpture in America has become an art in itself—and you are still leading others merrily along their way."

But Janet Scudder does not now confine herself merely to sculpture. Of late years she has painted pictures, and of course they are good pictures, so good that they have been placed in the Montross Art Galleries in New York. New York and Paris, these are the two cities that best know Janet Scudder and her work. Her fame is not confined to the cities, however—all America does her honor and France has made her a Chevalière de la Légion d'Honneur. The girl who has made her own name in sculpture is keeping right on making her name stand for what is worth while in life and in art.

CHAPTER X

ANNA HYATT HUNTINGTON, WHO LOVED HORSES

GREAT talents may sometimes be revealed in babyhood, but families may have no way of recognizing them. When little Anna Hyatt, still a toddler, was continually escaping to the stable to lie under the feet of the family horse in order, as she tried to explain, that she might watch his jaws work, certainly her anxious mother and nurse could not have prophesied that the little runaway would one day model one of the greatest equestrian statues of the world. Anna Hyatt showed her love of horses in her very first years, and throughout her brilliant career as a sculptor of animals she has never stopped loving them.

The child who was one day to make a statue that every visitor to New York passes as the bus rolls him up Riverside Drive, was born in Cambridge, Massachusetts, in 1876. It is not strange that very early she revealed an interest in animals that has been not merely artistic, but also scientific, for her father was Alpheus Hyatt, professor of zoölogy at Harvard, and friend of Agassiz. Down at the old sea-farm at Annisquam on Cape Ann, where the family spent their summers, one room of the old gray Colonial house, was fitted up as a marine laboratory. This humble home-laboratory of Anna Hyatt's childhood was destined to grow and to develop until it was moved to Wood's Hole and became a place now famous for scientific study.

Down at Seven Acres at Annisquam there were horses, of course, heavy, plodding work horses, for a little girl to watch, as they drew the plow or brought home the hay cut in the sea-meadows. There was another place where horses might be observed, horses of a very different kind. The Hyatts' ancestral home was at Hyattsville, Maryland, and from time to time members of the family sojourned there. There on the old plantation were to be found pictures of thoroughbreds. Before she could read, little Anna knew those pictures by heart. Later on, when she was grown up, there were still long periods passed in Maryland. There Anna Hyatt rode horses, raised horses, modeled horses, but always, riding, raising, modeling, she has preserved unbroken her first baby affection for her four-footed friends. No one can look today at one of Anna Hyatt's horses, whether it is some little shivering colt done in a tiny bronze, or whether it is the great heroic steed that Joan of Arc mounts on Riverside Drive, and not see that back of the sculptor is a woman who utterly understands the very heart of a horse.

But the little girl growing up in Cambridge did not know she was to be a sculptor, although she watched with growing interest the studies of an artistic older sister. For herself Anna, a pupil, meanwhile, at a private school, thought she wanted to be a violinist. As one reads the lives of artists, one is surprised to find how often music has been a preoccupation almost as strong as the impulse toward clay or paint or marble. Anna Hyatt gave herself so intensely to her violin that she suffered a complete and prolonged nervous breakdown, due to the long hours of practicing. It was one day during her convalescence that she took up a piece of her sister's clay and began modeling the great Dane who was house dog and family friend. It was one of those casual little happenings that sometimes change the course of a life. The untaught fingers had made the dog alive. They had discovered their destined ability. Anna Hyatt knew now, and knew forever, what she wanted to be. There were no more violin lessons, instead there were lessons in art in Boston with Henry Kitson.

From those early art-student days in Boston, Anna Hyatt's career has been one of steady advance. It was now, here in Boston, that wild animals first began to fascinate her. The Bostock shows with all their jungle life from time to time visited the staid old city for long periods. Anna got permission to be a constant visitor, and to model from the life as constantly. The danger didn't bother her. It was the play of muscle she was after, and the swift, stealthy movements she longed to catch and to convey to bronze. She was quite undaunted by the fact that a surly elephant, not able to kill her as he desired, contented himself with squirting dirty water over her. She was undeterred from her study of the great felines by the tiger who, reaching out a deadly paw, smashed her clay model instead of herself.

Although she has always studied with the great masters of her art, Anna Hyatt has always done a great deal of her work independent of instruction. She has done this by conviction, believing that an artist owes it to himself first to develop his own individuality, and not to let himself be influenced too early by other people, no matter how great those other people may be. It was this intention first to learn how to be herself in her own way that kept the budding sculptor in Boston before going on to New York, and then kept her for years in New York before going on for further study in France.

In New York, while she studied at the Art Students' League and with Gutzon Borglum, Anna Hyatt still for the most part pursued her independent path. Her wild-animal bronzes began to be known and favorably commented on by critics. Her wild-animal studies were continued in the Bronx Zoo, where visitors often showed as much interest in the slim fair girl modeling from the life so absorbedly, as they did in the wild creatures she was copying. The sinuous, treacherous movements of the jaguar were beginning to interest her intensely. Some of her best pieces represent the flashing action, or the stealthy approach of this animal so difficult to portray. There is one of a jaguar leaping to clutch with his teeth the outstretched wing of a struggling crane. Another famous treatment is known as the "Reaching Jaguars," a design for gateposts, representing two animals each with an evil paw extended down the side of the post.

The hours spent in close companionship with the splendor and the ferocity of the wild creatures of the Zoo, the engagements and the commissions now resulting from an increasing fame, were happily off-

set by the coziness of the domestic life in the studio
home in Twelfth Street. Anna Hyatt at first shared
an apartment with another young sculptor, Brenda
Putnam. There are accounts of delightful informal
Sunday afternoon *salons* presided over by Mrs.
Hyatt, come down from Cambridge. There are
evenings to be remembered when the mother would
read aloud, and the daughter's unceasing hands,
while she listened, would take up a bit of red modeling wax, and half unconsciously produce a tiny piece
of priceless art, perhaps a paper knife with one of
her favorite jaguars for a handle.

In 1904 Anna Hyatt was engaged for a time in
a most interesting partnership, an experiment in
collaboration with another woman sculptor, A. St.
Leger Eberle. The two had several things in common. Both had given up music for sculpture, both
were resolved to be independent students, not rush-
ing off to Paris for instruction, believing in the
inspiration of their own native America. The two
young women worked jointly at their groups, figures representing animals and human beings together, Miss Eberle doing the human figure, and
Miss Hyatt the animals. One of the best known of
the groups is "Men with Bull."

This partnership was presently dissolved, and
now the course that is inevitable for every artist,
no matter how long postponed, opened for Anna
Hyatt. Her reputation as an accomplished sculptor
was established. The power and the beauty com-
pressed into her little bronzes were known to all
lovers of art. Museums and private collectors recognized the range of her work, from the patient toil-

ing dray horses to fighting elephants or a poised tiger. Anna Hyatt's name had become famous as a sculptor of animals. She was known as the only woman sculptor to concentrate attention on wild beasts. But up to this time, on the eve of her long-delayed departure to foreign study, Anna Hyatt had never made a statue of the human figure.

For a time in France, as in her own United States, Miss Hyatt's concentration upon animal sculpture continued. In D'Aubigny's studio in Anvers-sur-Oise she made the great Danes now in the Metropolitan Museum. But later, in her own studio workshop in the Latin Quarter of Paris, a new interest began to touch her imagination, a new interest which was steadily to increase through the years and was destined to express itself at last in the greatest achievement of her genius. In France, where memories of the martyred Maid of Orléans crowd everywhere upon the attention, Miss Hyatt became more and more fascinated by the character of Joan of Arc, and yet it was actually the pen of an American that revealed the peasant girl of the fifteenth century to the sculptor girl of the twentieth. It was Mark Twain's life of Joan which made the long-dead peasant leader more and more a living reality to Anna Hyatt. With Mark Twain's conception of the character to guide her, Miss Hyatt looked at all the reminders of the Maid that came to her eye, and read the legends to be studied in every library. It is said that every sculptor in France does his Joan of Arc, but with few of these presentations of a popular heroine was Miss Hyatt satisfied. They showed the peasant girl of Domrémy too vigorous and earthy, or too military in her pomp, or perhaps too fragile and childish. More and more Anna Hyatt's imagination perceived the girl who heard voices and saw visions out of nowhere as a girl all flame and spirit and religious fervor. Three different statues of Joan of Arc Miss Hyatt has made, but all of them have been portraits of a girl's soul aflame with the unseen.

Two of the three statues are equestrian, and of these two the first was modeled in the Latin Quarter studio. It would be most interesting and noteworthy in itself, if it were not even more interesting and noteworthy, as being the forerunner of the much greater statue now overlooking the Hudson River. In any work of art it is an absorbing study to watch the development of an idea in an artist's mind. One can sometimes observe the earliest beginning of a musical theme or a literary one, or the first vision of a picture or a statue, as it steadily grows and deepens and is perfected by repeated patient experiment. Miss Hyatt's first Joan did not attain the grandeur of her second, but it pointed toward it. It also revealed the prodigious patience of her workmanship and her determination upon perfection. This statue marked a change, too, in the course of her career. There are critics who maintain that Anna Hyatt did not really enter into the fullness of her powers until she began to model the human figure.

Up to this time that love of horses revealed in her babyhood had been shown only in bronzes, marvelously alive but small. Joan of Arc must have a steed of warlike size, and the American sculptor began to look over Paris to find one. It must be no slim Arab steed, either, but a horse stout enough to bear a rider in fifteenth-century armor. Research had already revealed that in Joan's day the horse itself was not yet encased in metal. Search at last secured a magnificent Percheron in the delivery service of the Louvre stores. The store management gladly offered the splendid model for the sculptor's need, and while the work went on he was daily led out from the Louvre stables and across the Seine to the studio in the Latin Quarter.

Miss Hyatt exhibited her Joan of Arc in the Paris Salon of 1910. The judges awarded her a certificate of honorable mention, but apart from that polite acknowledgment of her ability they expressed a smiling doubt when the sculptor gave her account of her work. Such a piece of statuary must have taken years to accomplish, said the judges. It took exactly four months, said the young woman who had produced it, but it was four months of seven days a week and ten hours a day, and all absolutely without assistance. Still the judges were unconvinced, they even scoffed at her assertion that she had constructed the armature herself, that is, unaided, she had built the framework of iron and wood, which must, like a skeleton, underpin all the clay. While stoutly asserting her veracity, Anna Hyatt was forced to admit that it is, "a terribly brutal piece of work; massing on three and a half tons of clay does entail great physical labor."

But in spite of all its incredible toil this first treatment of Joan of Arc did not satisfy its creator. The hope of a better, greater rendering of the same theme continued to burn deep down in her mind, until, on her return to this country, something hap, pened to fan it once more aflame. It seemed that a little group of New York men and women had somehow found themselves drawn together by a common interest, their enthusiasm for a French peasant girl six centuries dead, but still altogether worthy of being made alive here in an alien land. This little band of her twentieth-century admirers were ashamed of the fact that this great American city had no statue of the Maid of Domrémy. They organized themselves into a committee, with J. Edgar Saltus, famous authority on Joan's tragic history, at its head. The committee's purpose was the securing of a statue of Joan of Arc of which they and the whole city might be proud, but they went about this purpose very quietly, very humbly, and very slowly, for they spent five whole years in the accomplishment of their aim. Quietly members of the committee spent years in independent research. Quietly some of them traveled to all the spots in France connected with Joan's story, and when the decision was reached to open a competition to the sculptors of the world, even the competition was not noisily advertised, but whispered. But somehow it became known so widely that the designs pouring in represented six different nationalities. A design that almost succeeded was by a Russian Jew. But it was Anna Hyatt's model that won first award in a competition "open to any artist, without restriction as to age or sex, religion, place of birth, or abode."

Now ensued that tense period in which the committee set itself to collect money for the erection of the statue-to-be, and in which the sculptor retired to put her successful design into its heroic shape. She went back to the old sea acres at Annisquam. Once again the securing of a horse suitable for a model became the first need. This time again it must be a horse of great size, great strength, and also of great beauty. The Gloucester fire department owned a horse that seemed in his magnificence to have been created for this very need. Every day he was brought to the sculptor's studio, the pride of the community that lent him.

War thunders were already rolling far off when on a day of 1915, in the presence of the French ambassador, the statue of the warrior girl of France upon her splendid mount was unveiled to the crowd. It stands on a little knoll at 93rd Street, overlooking the Hudson. In its pedestal are imbedded some of the actual stones taken from the dungeon at Rouen where Joan of Arc was imprisoned.

Miss Hyatt's New York Joan has been called "one of the few really monumental, impressive, and expressive equestrian statues of modern times." Of the labor that went to make the statue it has been said: "The work involved two very different requirements: a thorough knowledge of equine sculpture and a capacity to realize the spirit of the Maid. . . . Anna Hyatt was capable of both requirements. She knew horses, and though her previous groups had been small they promised the bigness and grandeur, as well as the big form and vigorous movement."

While there is great strength in the statue there is grace as well and flowing movement. Right forefoot lifted, head drawn back by the bridle, the large horse with his relatively small rider adds to her spirituality. The complete impression is of "spiritual possession." Joan does not brandish her sword, but fixes her eyes upon the cross on its hilt.

The gift of this statue to America's greatest city stands for a generous thoughtfulness on the part of the committee and gives promise of what other interested experts may in future days do for their community.

Made and erected in Miss Hyatt's own country, the statue of the French Maid yet brought recognition from France. In 1922 the French Government made Anna Hyatt a Chevalière of the Legion of Honor. A copy of the Manhattan Joan is now in Blois, France.

In 1923 the gifted young sculptor surprised the wide circle of her friends by marrying Archer M. Huntington, son of the railroad king, Collis P. Huntington, a gifted critic. Within a few months the newly married pair set out for a two years' journey in the South Seas. Their beautiful yacht was called *Rocinante*.

But travel did not make Anna Hyatt Huntington forget her love for clay and horses. She has turned of late for subjects to the romantic history of Spain. Her "Cid" shows a prancing horse and a magnificent mounted figure bearing an uplifted javelin.

So well has Mrs. Huntington succeeded in portraying Spanish subjects that the following announcement appeared in 1931, "The Academia de Bellas Artes of Madrid has elected to membership the sculptress Anna Hyatt Huntington, wife of

Archer M. Huntington, President of the Hispanic Society. This honor is in recognition of the work which Mrs. Huntington has done on behalf of Spain. She has recently presented the city of Palos with a commemorative statue of the Commandante Franco."

As well as France and Spain, her own native America has done honor to Anna Hyatt Huntington. Her work is in the Metropolitan Museum in New York. She is a member of the American National Academy, the National Sculpture Society, and the Federation of Arts. For some years Mrs. Huntington has been Curator of sculpture in the French Museum in New York City.

The little girl who loved horses and watched them has grown to be an internationally known sculptor, but no matter how far her fame carries her she will never outgrow her love for animals, for people, and for her art.

CHAPTER XI

MALVINA HOFFMAN,
SCULPTOR OF TYPES

SUPPOSE you were a sculptor and had a commission
—commission being the art word for job—and the
commission was not one, but over a hundred busts
and figures, wouldn't you feel busy? And then follow your imagination a little farther and try to
think that those busts and whole figures must be
types, not individuals, and that they can't possibly
be done in a home studio because the types are of
races of living men. The study of world races means
world travel for the sculptor.

Now this commission, which sounds so like a bit
of fairy fiction, has actually been given to the sculptor, Malvina Hoffman. What is more, she has accepted it, proving her energy and spirit as well as
her ability. Her finished work will be placed in the
Hall of Living Men of the Field Museum of Chicago. All these many pieces of sculpture will be a
permanent part of the art of America—and a
woman is making them.

What sort of a woman is she? What sort of a girl
was this Malvina Hoffman who has set out to study
and copy race types? She was a girl of old-time
New York. Her birth year was 1887. Malvina's
father was an English musician, a pianist, and a

friend of Jenny Lind's. In fact, Richard Hoffman knew most of the famous musicians of his time. Malvina was the youngest child and had much musical ability. She heard music and made music, but she liked painting and drawing even better than she liked the piano. She had art lessons from the famous portrait-painter, John Alexander. But, after teaching her painting for six years, he advised her to turn to sculpture. Her first bust was made when she was twenty-three years old. She took her father's handsome head for her subject, and she made her copy seem alive. "It is the bust of a man who listens, and who listens to inner voices."

It was the first of many portrait groups and figures. The girl who has always been so successful in reproducing other people's features had herself a very interesting face and head. It has been said that, "her portrait in some illustrated journal of that period shows a beautiful young girl with distinguished features; the eyes thoughtful, the mouth strong and superbly drawn, the glorious hair massed in two heavy coils, indicate the perfect type of active idealist. Plastically and intellectually she seems to have carved her own self."

At twenty-three, Malvina Hoffman had, besides her interesting appearance, many characteristics that gave promise of a distinguished life. She was greatly talented in art, she was an indomitable worker, and she was sure-willed. Best of all, she was a friend-maker. And once having made them, she kept her friends. Her affection for them endured as her chiseled statues endured, because there was a rock foundation.

Malvina needed her friend-making ability when, after her father's death, she went with her mother to Paris. Of course, the young sculptor went to the French capital to study, and equally a matter of course, she knew whom she wished for a teacher. It was no other than the great Rodin. Five times he refused to see her. At last, when she persisted in wishing to work in his studio, he looked at her drawings and allowed her to spend a day in his workroom, a day when he himself was absent. What epochal hours those proved to be for the young American girl! She realized her priceless privilege and filled her mind with the master's work. She tried to understand him. A few days later she brought Rodin the result of her studio study. He accepted her as his pupil.

The best proof that she was fitted to be Rodin's pupil is that she never copied her teacher but always understood him.

So well has she understood that the director of the Luxembourg enrolled her help for the arrangement of the Rodin Museum in the Hôtel Biron. It has been said that a great man's best pupils are those who follow his virtues without imitating his manner, who keep in this way their own individuality and the master's.

And Malvina Hoffman has always kept her own individuality; perhaps that is the reason she is so well able to portray the individuality in other people. She has made portraits of statesmen, thinkers, generals, and artists.

Many of Miss Hoffman's portrait studies are of her friends. She has made portraits of Paderewski.

Her own knowledge of music probably helped in both the portrait and the friendship-making. Neither was done quickly. "For more than a year before knowing him personally Malvina Hoffman studied Paderewski in various moods and under various circumstances. She watched him, for instance, during the conferences of the League of Nations in Geneva. She was able to understand him as a musician-statesman and as a delightful friend" —"a friend frank, witty, carrying into all subjects touched upon the impression of a man who has learned, felt, and understood much."

There are portrait studies of Malvina Hoffman's famous dancer friend, the great Pavlowa. Both women were artists, one in musical movement, one in marble; loving art, they loved and understood each other. This understanding attachment showed itself in a practical way—Malvina Hoffman took thirty lessons in the dance. Pavlowa posed hours on end so that the sculptor might have every advantage in doing her modeling. The result of this understanding friendship has been priceless to the world. There are a portrait mask in wax of the dead dancer, a marble bust and a polychrome relief called the Byzantine Madonna, as well as the wonderful paneled frieze, the "Russian Bacchanale," in which Miss Hoffman's portrait figures seem to move to music.

Malvina Hoffman has made many famous portrait studies—that of Sir David Henderson, Henry C. Frick, Mrs. Frick, Mrs. Harriman and others— all done in a spirit of friendship and sympathy that portrays the best in each individuality.

The sculptor's sympathy and human interest are
also shown in her treatment of humbler subjects.
"Bill Working" is a kneeling figure, clad in sleeve-
less shirt and overalls, pail at his side, squatted to
scrub. The "Coal Man" is characteristically carved
out of a block of anthracite. This figure is most interesting in a cowled cap, the face below bearded
and bowed like a gnome of a fairy tale, only larger.

Animals, too, have been Miss Hoffman's models.
There is her bronze of Kiki, a Siamese cat, seated
and dignified. There is also a splendid Arab stallion
statue, a rearing figure, trumpeting and alive.

The gifted sculptor has also made symbolic figures. "To the Friendship of English-speaking Peo-
ples" is a colossal group to be placed in London.
Miss Hoffman chiseled it in the United States from
Indiana limestone. In fact, chiseling and carving in
stone are what Malvina Hoffman likes to do. For
her magnificent work, "Sacrifice," she sent to Caen
for a block of stone weighing ten tons. She worked
on it in a hall lighted by one south window only.
In cutting the armor she used no hammer, merely
pressed her chisel into the stone for fear of break-
ing the fragile armor links. "Sacrifice" represents
the outstretched figure of a Crusader, his head upon
his mother's knee as she kneels beside him. The
effect of the whole is not agony, but repose. Malvina
Hoffman says of it, "Both are proud of their sacrifice, and ask neither pity nor sympathy."

This group, showing the best of the sculptor's art
and the best of her understanding sympathy, is
meant to commemorate the Harvard men killed in
the World War. It was given by Mrs. Robert

Bacon in memory of her husband, one-time ambassador to France.

In "Sacrifice," as in all her other sculpture, it has been said of Malvina Hoffman's work that, "a thought always commands and dominates it— whereas many sculptors are satisfied with no thought, or the thought of others."

In her busy, useful life many things besides fame have come to Malvina Hoffman. Foreign travel has been hers, and useful war relief work and marriage. She is now Mrs. Samuel B. Grimson. But wherever she travels and whatever happens to her, Malvina Hoffman is first of all the girl who followed her chisel to fame and who has won appreciation all over the earth. France has been especially interested in this pupil of Rodin's. The French critic Alexandre has written most understandingly of her art. America, in giving Malvina Hoffman the Field Museum commission, has shown that her own country appreciates to the full the woman who can make stone and bronze reflect her thoughts.